DREAMS OF A REFUGEE

DREAMS OF A REFUGEE

From the Middle East to Mount Everest

MOSTAFA SALAMEH

Edited by Robert Mullan

BLOOMSBURY

LONDON · OXFORD · NEW YORK · NEW DELHI · SYDNEY

Bloomsbury Continuum
An imprint of Bloomsbury Publishing Plc

50 Bedford Square
London
WC1B 3DP
UK

1385 Broadway
New York
NY 10018
USA

www.bloomsbury.com

Bloomsbury, Continuum and the Diana logo are trademarks of Bloomsbury
Publishing Plc

First published 2016
Paperback, 2017

British Library Cataloguing-in-Publication Data
A catalogue record for this book is available from the British Library.

Library of Congress Cataloguing-in-Publication data has been applied for.

ISBN: HB: 9781472927514
PB: 9781472943835
ePDF: 9781472927538
ePub: 9781472927521

2 4 6 8 10 9 7 5 3 1

Typeset by Integra Software Services Pvt. Ltd.
Printed and bound in Great Britain by CPI Group (UK) Ltd, Croydon CR0 4YY

To find out more about our authors and books visit www.bloomsbury.com.
Here you will find extracts, author interviews, details of forthcoming events and
the option to sign up for our newsletters.

…Allah will not change the condition of a people until they change what is in themselves.

Qur'an, 13:11

If you can talk with crowds and keep your virtue,
Or walk with Kings – nor lose the common touch;
If neither foes nor loving friends can hurt you;
If all men count with you, but none too much;
If you can fill the unforgiving minute
With sixty seconds' worth of distance run,
Yours is the Earth and everything that's in it,
And – which is more – you'll be a Man, my son!

Rudyard Kipling

For my parents

CONTENTS

LIST OF ILLUSTRATIONS

1. Mostafa Salameh aged three with his father and brother, Rafat.

2. At a school party, 1986.

3. Graduation day from Queen Margaret University, Edinburgh in 2000.

4. Working for the Jordanian ambassador in London, Belgravia Place, 1993.

5. Mostafa's mother and father in Kuwait, 1988.

6. Mostafa in Nepal, 2013.

7. With Mazen Al Saher in Luton, 1995.

8. At the wedding of a friend, Mark Porter, with Simon Dunn, 2004.

9. Mostafa with Mark Manley, Everest Base Camp, 2007.

10. At Marcello's Restaurant in Hitchin, 1997.

11. Stephen Torsi, his mother Denise and father Toni, Christmas 1996.

12. At the top of Denali, the highest point in North America, 12th June 2004.

13. At the dentist, Namche Bazaar, Nepal, May 2008.

14. The cover of *JO* magazine (Jordan), February 2004.

15. Mostafa with Dr Mike Stroud, Cho Oyu, Tibet, 2007.

16. Mostafa climbing an ice fall on Mount Everest, 2008.

17. The Hillary Step, Mount Everest.

FOREWORD

It has been my great pleasure to become acquainted with the Jordanian mountaineer, author and activist Mostafa Salameh over the past twelve years. Some time ago, Mostafa shared with me his dream to climb Mount Everest for the benefit of Jordan and as a role model for Arab youth. In completing this challenge he would become the first Jordanian to conquer Everest, before going on to scale the Seven Summits and reach both Poles. I was delighted when on May 25th 2008, Jordan's Independence Day, Mostafa called me early in the morning to convey the splendid news that he had summited Mount Everest. He has since accomplished the rest of his objectives – the Explorer's 'Grand Slam' – and with this book has added to those achievements once more.

With his deep understanding for the challenges that refugees face and dedication to his work with young people across the Middle East and the World encouraging them to pursue their dreams, Mostafa is a truly remarkable individual. I feel strongly that Mostafa Salameh's story should be read for its larger message on the determination necessary to face real challenges and make a change for the better.

His Majesty King Abdullah II ibn Al Hussein
The Hashemite Kingdom of Jordan
September 2016

PREFACE

2017 – Climbing Ben Nevis for the People of Palestine

*I am proud of my Muslim beliefs and I am proud of
my Jordanian identity, and I am proud of the Palestinian blood
that runs in my veins, and I am proud of being British.*
MOSTAFA SALAMEH

Sometime in November 2017, on the hundredth anniversary of the Balfour Declaration, I'll be taking a group of about twenty people, from various countries of the Arab World, to the peak of Ben Nevis. On this legendary Scottish mountain I'll unfurl the Palestinian flag and also that of the BDS movement, a Palestinian civil society-led group calling for 'boycotts, divestment and sanctions' against Israel until it complies with international law. In doing so I will try and raise awareness of the injustices continuously meted out to Palestinians both in their homeland and in the many refugee camps scattered among its neighbouring countries.

My companions will be Palestinians from around the world, including the USA, Europe and the Occupied West Bank. Among them will be academics, artists and journalists – all people who can communicate to the world what has been achieved and why the climb took place. I found many of these enthusiastic Palestinians through Facebook, others through my informal networks, and some through my great friend Mary Nazzal-Batayneh, a barrister and activist for Palestinian rights. The climb will be sponsored and we will raise money for numerous Palestinian causes.

I climb mountains for a cause, not just for the thrill and sense of adventure.

Ben Nevis (Gaelic: *Beinn Nibheis*) is indisputably the highest mountain in Britain. *Beinn* is the most common Gaelic word for mountain, while *Nibheis* is usually translated as 'malicious' or 'venomous'. An alternative interpretation is that *Beinn Nibheis* derives from '*beinn nèamh-bhathais*', from '*nèamh*' ('heavens, clouds') and '*bathais*' ('top of a man's head'); in other words, the mountain with its head in the clouds or, indeed, the mountain of Heaven.

At 1,344 metres (4,409 feet) above sea level, it's found at the western end of the Grampian Mountains, close to the small but well-known town of Fort William. It's a popular destination, attracting well over 100,000 ascents a year, most of whose climbers use the Pony Track from Glen Nevis. The 700-metre (2,300 feet) cliffs of the north face are among the highest in the UK, and provide classic scrambles and rock climbs of all levels of difficulty for mountaineers. The summit is the collapsed dome of an ancient volcano, and features the ruins of an observatory, which was in continuous use between 1883 and 1904. The data collected during this period are still important for understanding Scottish mountain weather and, indeed, Charles Wilson invented his cloud chamber after a period spent working there.

The first path to the peak was built at the same time as the observatory and designed to allow ponies to carry up supplies, with a maximum gradient of one in five. The path made the ascent popular, all the more so after the arrival in 1894 of Fort William's West Highland Railway.

The first recorded ascent of Ben Nevis was made on 17 August 1771 by Edinburgh botanist James Robertson, who was in the region collecting specimens. John Keats reached the peak in 1818, and compared the ascent to 'mounting ten St Paul's without the convenience of a staircase.'[1] The following year, the naturalist William MacGillivray reached the summit only to find what he described as 'fragments of earthen and glass ware, chicken bones, corks, and bits of paper.'[2] It was not until 1847 that the Ordnance Survey confirmed Ben Nevis as the highest mountain in Britain and Ireland, ahead of its rival Ben Macdhui.

When I proudly stand on Ben Nevis, I will say, 'This is the hundredth anniversary of the Balfour Declaration, and as I stand here on the top of Britain, I ask the British Government – what are you doing to solve the tragedy that your ancestors created?'

Very few documents in political history have had as much influence as the Balfour Declaration,[3] a 67-word statement contained within a short letter from the British Foreign Secretary, Lord Arthur Balfour, on 2 November 1917. This short declaration acknowledged the establishment of a Jewish home in Palestine.

His Majesty's Government view with favour the establishment in Palestine of a national home for the Jewish people, and will use

---

[1]Peter Hodgkiss (1994), *The Central Highlands*, Scottish Mountaineering Trust, p. 117.
[2]Andrew Hunter (2014), 'Bones on Ben Nevis – a walk back into history', *Leopard Magazine*, pp. 30–34.
[3]For an extensive and illuminating discussion of the Balfour Declaration, see Jonathan Schneer (2012), *The Balfour Declaration: The Origins of the Arab–Israeli Conflict*, London: Bloomsbury.

their best endeavours to facilitate the achievement of this object, it being clearly understood that nothing shall be done which may prejudice the civil and religious rights of existing non-Jewish communities in Palestine, or the rights and political status enjoyed by Jews in any other country.

The letter was addressed to Lionel Walter Rothschild, a British banker and Zionist activist, who drafted the declaration with the help of fellow Zionists Chaim Weizmann and Nahum Sokolow. The declaration proved to be in line with the wishes of Zionist leaders who hoped for a homeland in Palestine and the right for Jews from the world over to relocate there. Balfour was part of David Lloyd George's liberal government, which believed that Jews had undergone injustice for too long and that the West was to blame. Therefore, he reasoned, it was their responsibility to locate and establish a Jewish homeland.

The motivation for achieving this was aided by fundamentalist Christians who encouraged the depopulation of Jews *from their own lands*, and also wished to fulfil what they argued was the biblical prophecy, in which the return of Christ will occur after the establishment of 'a Jewish kingdom in the Holy Land'.

The Declaration was highly controversial, primarily because of the nature of its highly ambiguous and, perhaps, contradictory text. One interpretation was that what was being argued for was not the idea of establishing a unique Jewish state, but rather a geographical homeland where Jews would live alongside Palestinians and other Arabs. Also, it was pointed out that they could take the second part of the Declaration, concerning the protection of the rights of Palestinian Arabs, as the British endorsing Arab autonomy. Britain indeed protected Arab rights at some points during the mandate, but its role remained contradictory.

In 1917, at the time of the Declaration, the Palestinian community numbered 90 per cent of the total population of Palestine, while Jews amounted to less than 10 per cent, some 50,000 in total. By the time of Israel's declaration of independence in 1947, the Jewish population had increased to 600,000 and had been busily establishing quasi-governmental institutions that, in turn, provoked resistance from Palestinians, which took the form of minor uprisings in 1920, 1921, 1929 and 1933 and the major 'Arab Revolt' which lasted from 1936 to 1939. This 'revolt' demonstrated that there could be no compromise between the two rival communities and that only a full-blown war could settle the issue. As the Jewish community was militarily weak it would have easily been defeated, had Britain not intervened. As Avi Shlaim has remarked, 'The Jewish national home, in the last resort, had to be defended by British bayonets.'[4]

As I mentioned earlier, the Declaration laid the foundation for the formation of the State of Israel, which, in 1948, finally appeared some thirty-one years later. One of the Declaration's fiercest critics has been the late eminent Palestinian scholar Edward Said, who, in *The Question of Palestine*, describes the Declaration's unspoken assumptions. The 'imperialistic Declaration', he writes, was made:

(a) by a European power, (b) about a non-European territory, (c) in flat disregard of both the presence and the wishes of the

---

[4]Avi Shlaim, 'The Balfour Declaration and its Consequences', in Roger Louis, ed. (2005), *Yet More Adventures with Britannia: Personalities, Politics and Culture in Britain*, London: I. B. Tauris.

native majority resident in the territory, and (d) it took the form
of a promise about this same territory to another foreign group, so
that this foreign group might, quite literally, make this territory a
national home for the Jewish people.[5]

The Balfour Declaration might well be termed, remarks Avi Shlaim,
'the first or original sin'.[6] In Arabic there's a saying that something that
starts crooked, remains crooked.

To be clear: the Balfour Declaration was ambiguous in terms of
language and intention – the 'national home' it promised to the Jews
was never clearly defined and, besides, there wasn't any precedent in
international law. On the other hand, it was arrogant, dismissive and
even racist, to refer to 90 per cent of the population as 'the non-Jewish
communities in Palestine'.[7] It was the worst kind of double standard,
implying that there was one law for the Jews, and a different one for
everyone else.

Britain had no moral mandate to promise national rights for a tiny
Jewish minority in a predominantly Arab country. Moreover, at no
stage in this long saga did the Jews feel that they were getting from their
great sponsor the support to which they felt entitled, and the Arabs
were violently opposed to the Balfour Declaration from the very start.
They held Britain responsible for the loss of their patrimony to the
Jewish intruders. By the end of the mandate, there was no gratitude
and no goodwill left towards Britain on either side of the Arab–Jewish
divide. Shlaim concludes:

---

[5]Edward W. Said (1979), *The Question of Palestine*, New York: Random House, pp. 15–16.
[6]Shlaim (2005).
[7]*Ibid.*

...the Balfour Declaration was a colossal blunder – it has proved to be a catastrophe for the Palestinians and it gave rise to one of the most intense, bitter, and protracted conflicts of modern times.[8]

*

I was born to Palestinian refugees. Their struggle against injustice and for freedom has shaped my life. But I have refused to live anything less than a fulfilling, adventurous and free life. I hope my story will inspire people, including Palestinians, to break any proverbial chains and follow *their* dreams.

---

[8] *Ibid.*

1

Childhood

All that we can hope for is that a day will come, when we have all gone, when people will say that this man has tried, and his family tried. This is all there is to seek in this world.
KING HUSSEIN I OF JORDAN

To be born an Arab is the only perfect crime in this age!
MUHAMMAD AL-MAGHUT

My parents met in the Palestinian refugee camp al-Wihdat, in Amman, Jordan, which is sometimes known as the Amman New Camp. It was established in 1948, and now houses over 50,000 registered refugees. There are high levels of unemployment and poverty in the camp, evident to anyone who visits, and where men of all ages eagerly look for work.

They were introduced through my dad's best friend, who was my mum's brother. Sadly, at about the time of their marriage, my mum's brother was killed in a clash between the PLO (Palestinian Liberation Organization) and the Jordanian Army. He was immediately buried in al-Wihdat, but then later moved and buried elsewhere.

Almost two million Palestinian refugees live in Jordan, with approximately 338,000 in camps. Most Palestinian refugees have been granted Jordanian citizenship, unlike in Lebanon, where they remain aliens without citizenship or any meaningful rights.

Whenever I return to Amman I meet up with my dad and visit al-Wihdat, where I spent a few years of my childhood. I vividly remember when, as a seven-year-old boy, my mum would send me to buy vegetables, and I'd be served by a friendly woman. Many years later, in 2015, I visited that same market and there was that woman, standing in the very same place she had been some thirty odd years earlier. I immediately recognised her voice, her kind manner and beautiful gentle face. The population was greater in those days, but much of the camp and the busy market remains the same.

Al-Wihdat is within walking distance of bustling and vibrant downtown Amman. There are no fences, walls or barbed wire separating the camp from the rest of the city. Because of the traffic congestion on some of the overcrowded main streets, pollution is thick and greater than in the rest of Amman. Palestinian refugees are allowed access to public services and healthcare, and, as a result, refugee camps are becoming more like poor inner-city districts. There are over two thousand small enterprises in the camp, and at the beginning of the 1990s these enterprises were mainly small, simple, family-owned businesses with a low level of technical expertise. But today they include banks, jewellers, pharmacies, travel agencies, electronics shops, as well as a huge number of grocers, clothing stores, vegetable shops and, invariably, fast food outlets.

My granddad lived in the Az-Zarqā refugee camp, in the north of Jordan.[1] Death was always present in my family, and my grandma died suddenly and inexplicably. My dad was one of eight children and had four brothers and three sisters. His father re-married after his wife suddenly died, and his new wife already had eight sons and six daughters of her own, so life was pretty chaotic.

My mum and dad moved to Kuwait, in the hope of a better life. My mum had already experienced difficulties: her own mother had died when she was quite young and her father had re-married. In Kuwait my dad worked numerous different jobs, including as a salesman in various retails outlets, especially in the garment trade; then as a driving instructor, teaching people to drive; but, most of the time, he worked as a lorry driver. The journeys he undertook in his huge and uncomfortable vehicle were long and consisted, mainly, of trips to Germany and Iraq.

They settled in Salmiya (As-Sālmīya), a city in the Hawalli Governorate in Kuwait. The city is divided into 12 blocks, and the blocks located closer to the interior of the district tend to be residential, while those by the Persian Gulf coastline are more commercial and include some upmarket residential real estate. The interior residential areas boast a huge population of those from the Indian sub continent and other Arabs not native to the Persian Gulf. Although I remember Salmiya as quite a small city, it was home to many mosques, an aquarium, a scientific centre, a football stadium, a Roman Catholic chapel, the district passport office (Jawazat), a well-equipped park

---

[1] The city of Zarka has the second-largest population in Jordan – after Amman – with a total of around 500,000. The camp itself was established in 1949 and has a population of around 20,000.

beside the 5th Ring Road and, nowadays, I believe it proudly possesses an IMAX cinema. Notable malls include the Salmiya Souq mega-mall, which was Kuwait's first, Marina Mall in the Marina World shopping and entertainment district, and the well-known Omariya.

*

I was born in Kuwait, on 25 June 1970. I have seven brothers and two sisters, and I'm the second born. My siblings are Rafat, the oldest, Medhat (who now lives in Wales), Mamdouh (resident in Sweden), Bilal (also in Sweden), Saadeh (in Amman), Sabha (my sister, in Amman), Mohamed (who lives and works in London), Samya (my other sister, also in Sweden) and my youngest brother, Salameh (in Amman), aged 17.

Because of my dad's travelling and absence from home, my courageous and hardworking mum raised us alone. It was very difficult and was made worse when Rafat, my older brother, was hit by a bus as he crossed the road when he was just six, and I was five. My dad told the bus driver, 'Don't worry, it was our fault because he ran across the road.' As he was also a driver, my dad didn't want the driver to get into trouble or lose his job.

The head injury Rafat suffered rendered him speechless and for a long time he seemed to revert to infancy. In fact, after very little improvement, he's never really worked and has suffered long-term consequences. Interestingly enough, when my parents decided to try and marry him to a distant Palestinian cousin, she was greatly surprised when she met him for the first time, as she hadn't been told anything about his neurological state. Nevertheless, they eventually married and produced two beautiful children!

I've continually tried to help him, especially as he's been unable to earn a living. Indeed, I've always been called 'the oldest' because I've taken care of things and, as well as helping Rafat, I've also helped some of my other brothers get into the UK. Rafat and his wife now stay with my parents, in Amman.

I remember Kuwait as being incredibly hot. We lived, like other Palestinians, in a conventional housing block. Every block contained ten apartments, each with a mere two rooms, and in each block there were at least a hundred children, as well as many adults. There was nowhere to play and nowhere to go. We were all crammed in together. In fact, we slept on top of each other in an old and uncomfortable set of bunk beds. We had no shower facilities and so washed with water poured from buckets, and then once a week my mum would give each of us a shower, cleaning all the sand and dirt from our bodies. She kept the house spotless and I remember that she was forever cleaning.

My childhood, like most children's I suspect, was pleasant enough, not particularly dramatic and with no great highs and lows (with the exception of Rafat's accident). However, I soon realised I was a second-class citizen. Regularly and publicly I was called a 'Belgique', the specific term of abuse some Kuwaitis used against Palestinians, which some say originated from the country of Belgium being historically pro-Palestinian. I became aware that I actually attended different schools from ordinary Kuwaiti children. In my family we went to school in shifts; some of us went in the morning and the others after lunch. My family was poor but proud. There was never any spare money. As children and as a family we just about got what we needed, but it truly was a life of struggle. When I was a teenager it would take a month of saving any money I could find to go to McDonald's to buy a single burger, but never any dessert. Both my parents were strict and my dad would occasionally hit me, but only when he felt I 'deserved' it. Yet there was also so much laughter, so much fun, and my parents were proud of us and unconditionally loving towards us.

As I mentioned, there was nowhere to play, except in the street where we could kick a ball. On Thursdays we might collect as many onions and potatoes as we could and go out into the street and cook a barbecue. Sadly, swimming at the local public pool cost too much, so there were never any regular visits there.

*

My parents weren't religious, and hand-on-heart I can honestly say that I never ever went to the mosque with my dad, even on a Friday. When I did go it would be because of the extra-curricular trips they occasionally organised for children and families, such as swimming. As a treat, on a Friday, we would sometimes go with my mum or dad to the desert, or even further, to the seaside.

I never ever heard the term *jihad* used at home, at school or on the street, and similarly never heard the terms *Sunni* or *Shia*. At school what passed for 'religious education' consisted of each child reciting the *Qur'an*, without understanding much, if any, of what was actually being said. If we got any of the passages wrong we'd receive a painful slap across the face. At school we learned nothing of any real value about Islam, let alone any other religion.

*

At the age of 18 every Palestinian had to find a Kuwaiti sponsor, for some sort of education, training or employment, and if they failed to do so, they would have to leave the country. Any thought of a Palestinian entering a university was pointless. But I must say that Kuwait was good to me and gave me a basic primary education. However, when I reflect on my early years, I keep asking myself the question: 'Kuwait, you gave us schooling, why didn't you grant us any *rights*?'

Despite my early struggles, the racism and prejudice, my self-confidence began to take shape despite my lowly status, as I looked around at some of the Palestinians who left for America to prosper. Their families subsequently thrived through the money sent regularly to them from the US and elsewhere.[2] I took their victories as a sign that, despite being Palestinian, I too could leave the country and achieve elsewhere. This was perhaps a partly unconscious thought, but it certainly was there in my mind.

*

When I was a very young and naïve 18-year-old, with a sad and heavy heart, I left my family and Kuwait for the journey west to Jordan. We had very little money, so I couldn't afford a plane ticket, instead making the journey on an uncomfortable, overcrowded and stifling hot bus.

I was on my own, and hated it, mainly because I had to live with an aunt who I'd never previously met – and, of course, I missed my family. I was a normal 18-year-old, with the usual interests and preoccupations, so naturally I wanted a room of my own.

My aunt's name was Intisar. She had 18 children of her own, and when I lived with her 14 of them were still in the house. There were so many of us that I used to sleep outside, on the open roof. I subsequently moved out of my aunt's house and lived in the Al Hashmi Al-Shamali district of Amman, which was home to many Palestinians. I rented

---

[2] Remittances are of great importance for the economies of such countries as the Lebanon.

a room in a house which was actually a converted small loft. But I decorated it and made it nice and homely. I needed to somehow create that sense of 'family'.

Soon after I decided that I needed some sort of education and training, and so enrolled at the Ammon (with an 'o') College for Hospitality and Tourism. Now called the Jordan Applied University College of Hospitality and Tourism Education (JAU), it was always the best university-level college that specialised in Hospitality and Tourism Management training. It was established in 1980 and has always enjoyed a high profile among educational institutions in the Middle East. My dad had no money to send me to an actual university, but Ammon was cheap, and it was possible to enrol.

While I was a student I worked in many cafés and restaurants, first as a barman, then as a waiter. And despite having a Jordanian passport – the Jordanian government policy was to allow Palestinians to work and travel, so they wouldn't become a burden – I wasn't really getting anywhere, and of course it didn't help that I didn't have sufficient *wasta*, the connections with those in government and society that make life for some in Jordan easier.[3] I didn't know anyone, and didn't have any real influence. The gap between the rich and the poor in Jordan was huge, so this lack of *wasta* made my situation even worse.

I'd like to mention the fact that my dad, however, was not without political and cultural ambition. Despite working as a lorry driver he also produced small-scale Palestinian plays and, occasionally, directed

---

[3]See Robert B. Cunningham and Yasin K. Sarayrah (1993), *Wasta: The Hidden Force in Middle Eastern Society*, London: Praeger.

them. To put it in context, it should be remembered that in the 1970s and 80s Palestinian theatre was considered a small form of resistance as well as a source of national identity. Palestinian 'theatre' was, in fact, the theatre of the PLO (Palestinian Liberation Organization). My dad and his numerous and equally enthusiastic friends founded a theatre group, firstly in Kuwait. Then when he moved to Jordan he continued and would do everything – act, direct, produce, paint the scenery, and anything else that needed to be done. However, he also had to be extremely careful about what he said.

Again, it's important to remember the wider context: from 1948 onwards, Palestinians were forced to choose between accepting the blue Israeli ID card, or leaving the homeland and living as refugees outside the country, along with the rest of their brothers and sisters displaced in camps all around the world. Since Palestinian theatre was under the authority of the state where it existed, namely Israel, my dad, like many others, worked hard to ensure that it nonetheless remained *Palestinian* theatre, with its own identity, closely related to its Palestinian roots and Arabism.

From the late 1960s, particularly in the mid-1970s, there was a Palestinian and Arab creative awakening in many cultural and national fields, including theatre. Despite strict Israeli control there were theatre troupes in many villages, including Al-Masrah Al-Nahid of Haifa, Al-Masrah Al-Hadith in the city of Nazareth, and some in the (Arab) city of Jerusalem from the 1970s, until eventually the famous Palestinian Al-Hakawati Theatre was established.

By the second half of the 1980s, numbers of art and theatre enthusiasts had grown significantly. Many enrolled in higher education institutes and earned certificates. The field thrived. Today there are around twenty troupes and theatres, most of which receive subsidies from the Israeli Ministry of Culture. There are almost no independent theatres that don't receive subsidies from governmental institutions, aside from the one or two who refuse to work with them.

Nevertheless, the unequal distribution of subsidies to Palestinian troupes and theatres has unveiled the discrimination based on political affiliations. Almost 97 per cent of subsidies go to Jewish theatres and troupes, while only 3 per cent is allocated to Arabs. The budget is initially collected in the form of taxes and payments to public Israeli institutions. If we Palestinians currently constitute 20 per cent of the population, logically the state should give us back 20 per cent of the theatre-allocated budget.

*

At the end of 1990, my mum and dad, along with my siblings, left Kuwait at the time of the first Gulf War[4] and joined me in Jordan. When I found out they were planning to join me, I searched for somewhere for us all to live together and eventually found a flat within Amman's First Circle.

Dad lost all his money in Kuwait; in fact he lost everything, including all his personal possessions, the lorries he had bought, all the furniture; everything the family owned. He was in the PLO and my brother was a *fedayeen*, a Palestinian freedom fighter,[5] and had trained in Libya. So at the time of the Gulf War they were

[4]The war started on 2 August, when 100,000 Iraqi troops invaded Kuwait, and ended on 28 February 1991.
[5]For a discussion on the history of the *fedayeen*, see François Burgat (2003), *Face to Face with Political Islam*, London: I. B. Tauris.

understandably worried about any possible consequences of their fiercely held political beliefs and affiliations. My mum and dad left quickly and took everyone in the family with them.

*

When we lived in Kuwait we would occasionally visit distant relatives in Jordan, and also travel to Iraq – in particular Baghdad, where dad had many friends – and at the time we believed that Jordan was a desirable place to live. It was desirable, but being a refugee and being poor meant that there were always struggles.

Despite all my family being together in Jordan, in my heart I wanted to leave, to find a better life somewhere else. In particular I dreamt of living in England, although the 'England' I imagined owed much to the pages of Shakespeare. I knew that if I reached 'the white cliffs of Dover' my life would change. Serendipity came in the form of a meeting with Mohammad Adwan, who worked as an advisor to Jordan's King Hussein. His wife was American and she enjoyed my mum's cooking, so, as a consequence, my mum would occasionally send dishes and plates of food round to their house. And I would sometimes cater for them when they hosted large events. At one of these events I met the brother of the Jordanian ambassador in London, who said that his brother was looking for someone to work in the kitchen of his London house. I immediately said, 'OK, I want that job.'

2

London

Do not go where the path may lead; go instead where there is no path and leave a trail.

RALPH EMERSON

Bad days happen to everyone, but when one happens to you, just keep doing your best and never let a bad day make you feel bad about yourself.

BIG BIRD (SESAME STREET)

So in 1992 I left the long, hot, dry summers of Jordan and went to work as a dishwasher in the kitchen at the Jordanian embassy, in rainy and cold London. For my first few months there I was constantly wowed. It was amazing; all so shiny and new and completely different. I loved it.

Soon after I arrived, my brother Medhat followed, and for a very brief time he worked as a chef in the embassy's kitchen.

I wanted *change*. I wanted a different life to the one I had in Jordan. I wanted to learn new ways of working, new ways of thinking, and a new language. So it didn't take too long for me to become frustrated at learning very little; indeed, at times I felt that I was learning nothing.

Occasionally I felt as if I were merely living in a prison, like in Jordan, but instead in the UK.

My wages of £500 a month went straight to my dad in Amman, administratively channelled through the Ministry of Foreign Affairs. All I would personally receive in my pocket was £10 on each Sunday, before being unceremoniously kicked out of the embassy for the day. I didn't have any English language skills, which I craved, and the only language I would hear at the embassy was Arabic. For example, the Sri Lankan woman I worked with, the Filipino driver, the Pakistani gardener, all spoke to me exclusively in Arabic. A kind of epiphany occurred when, one dreary Sunday afternoon, I wandered over to Speakers' Corner. Here, for the first time in my life, I heard free speech. It was with astonishment that I discovered that British people were allowed to say whatever they wished.

*

Speakers' Corner[1] is one of Britain's most well-known places for public debate, often seen as a shining symbol of Britain's earlier entry into liberal democracy. The official story of its origins is a familiar one. It is argued that the Royal Parks and Gardens Regulation Act of 1872 allowed a space in the northeastern corner of Hyde Park to be given over for public speaking. A considerable debt for the passing of the Act is owed to the activities of the Reform League, which had pushed the question of the right to speak freely in Hyde Park. Thousands turned up to one such meeting on 23 July 1866, and when they found their access to the park blocked by over two thousand

---

[1] See John Roberts, *Tyburn Hanging Tree and the Origins of Speakers' Corner*, www. speakerscorner.net

policemen, they broke through and then debated political issues. As a consequence, parliamentary discussions followed about the right for 'free speech in Hyde Park'.

*

I particularly remember an Iraqi guy who would speak loudly and enthusiastically, sometimes aggressively, in defence of Saddam Hussein. He argued that there was a great conspiracy against Saddam and that, actually, instead of persecuting (and murdering) people he was the only person capable of holding the country together. There would also be Kurdish people talking, as well as Christians and other Muslims. I found it so interesting that people could say whatever they felt about their own country, even violently criticising the Prime Minister if they wished, something you could never do in the Arab world. And remember, many of these people were refugees, not actual UK citizens. A lot of the time I'd be listening to Arabic speakers, so my English language skills remained quite poor.

*

Meanwhile, at the embassy, things had taken a turn for the worse. The ambassador's American wife was neither a polite nor a friendly person. In fact, she treated embassy staff appallingly. The atmosphere was always tense: partly as a result of the ambassador's children, both of whom were regularly unwell. There was always tension. On a number of occasions and over a few different issues, I'd clashed with the ambassador himself. After one particularly strong disagreement between me and his wife, the ambassador stormed into my small living space. His face contorted with rage as he shouted angrily, 'While you're in this building you're actually in *Jordan*, don't think for a minute that you're in *Britain*.' He came closer, his hot breath in my face, and added, 'I could shoot you inside this embassy and no one would ever know.' After he left I stayed in my small room, a little shaken, and knew that I had to leave. The following day I informed the ambassador of my decision and he tried to talk me out of it. But my mind was set.

My visa had another four weeks to run, and thereafter I would receive a National Insurance number, which was very important. I decided that although I had to leave, I'd disappear back to Jordan for three weeks and then return just prior to the time when the visa would expire. While I was strategising and considering all the various options, the embassy's driver knocked on my door and drove me to Heathrow. Without even a backward glance he put me on a plane destined for Amman and walked away.

Though I left the embassy, I must recall a great memory. It was at the embassy that I first met the late King Hussein of Jordan. He was a humble man: he arrived at the embassy driving his own car! I served him coffee and felt proud and honoured to shake his hand.

As a result of the embassy debacle, I left and enjoyed a three-week family holiday in Amman, and then – again with a heavy heart – returned to the bleak surroundings of Heathrow and yet another rainy day!

Despite my monthly wages, my family had very little to give me, as all of the money I had sent them only just covered the costs of their food and accommodation. There was nothing left, nothing for any savings. So, on my return, I had a total of £80 in my pocket. When interrogated by Heathrow immigration officials, who asked for my 'papers', I decided to play dumb and suggest they contact 'my employer', the Jordanian embassy. It did the trick: perhaps because of the mention of the embassy, perhaps because I looked honest, or perhaps because it was a rainy day, or because it was a Friday afternoon and close to their clocking-off time, the officials simply waved me through. This was the start of living in the UK as an illegal immigrant for over twelve years.

*

As I mentioned, I had very little money. Perhaps more significantly, I had nowhere to live and no job. So what would I do? In steady drizzle, I stood outside Heathrow Airport waiting for Allah to give me a sign. Then, after a few fruitless minutes trying to think of a solution, I decided to get a taxi, as I'd heard of a hostel in South London favoured by Palestinians. The friendly driver was called Salah, another Palestinian, studying computer science and also driving a taxi. I said I'd heard of this hostel, but before I could give him the address he said he had a house in Putney, where he lived alone, and he also said that he'd quite like some company. 'Why don't you stay with me until you get yourself sorted?' Despite never having met him before, I seized the opportunity.

Salah was very smart, intelligent and kind. He owned a small two-bedroomed house in Putney. This was 1993, and at that time, of course, it was easy to rent and easy to buy. Salah worked the night shift and so would be out every evening and through the night. He was a very easygoing person.

As I settled in Putney I could hardly believe my good luck, and the following day I started looking for work. After a couple of frustrating and fruitless days, I stumbled into an East Sheen restaurant called the Naked Turtle and asked if there was any work. I was told to speak to the owner, Sami Bishlawi, a Palestinian who, after 1948, had gone to live in the United States, where he married an American woman. Later he came to England and opened the restaurant. I told him I needed a job, but admitted I couldn't speak English. Sami said I could work in the kitchen. I could tell that he really wanted to help me.

The job was simple and straightforward – I washed plates in the kitchen. After a short while I was moved and tended the bar, and later I worked front of house at the tables. Though some of the staff felt that Sami was slightly odd, perhaps a little forward, he was very kind to me and I was grateful for the opportunity to work in the restaurant.

While I worked in the kitchen, slowly but surely my English – both speaking and reading – improved. Every morning I'd arrive at the restaurant early, and stick some verbs and other things on to a board above the sink. I'd also read the *Sun*, which was the easiest newspaper to read – only later did I learn that it was also the worst! What really helped with my improvement in understanding and speaking English, however, was my daily habit of watching the TV show *Sesame Street*.

This legendary children's show first premiered in 1969 and used elements of commercial TV, such as music, humour and a strong visual style. The producers also used animation and short live-action films. With its crazy slapstick humour, *Sesame Street* became incredibly popular, not just in the US but all across the globe. When the show's producers decided to build a new format around an inner-city brownstone to appeal to urban children, they created Muppets that could interact with the human actors, specifically Oscar the Grouch and Big Bird, who became two of the show's most enduring characters.[2] These new episodes were directly responsible for what writer Malcolm Gladwell called 'the essence of *Sesame Street* – the artful blend of fluffy monsters and earnest adults'.[3]

And, yes, it was this unique and crazy show that helped me learn – while I was in my twenties! – to understand the English language as well as some of its idiosyncrasies.

*

So, my work chronology was as follows: from 1993–96, I worked one year in the Naked Turtle's kitchen and two years in the bar and restaurant. I earned good money, especially as I was popular and so received lots of tips, but I couldn't open a bank account because I was an illegal. My passport was due for renewal and of course I had no visa. All I had was my National Insurance number, which was valuable for work, but not for a bank account. Sami, however, had other ideas and persuaded a local NatWest 'bank manager friend' to allow me to open an account with my Jordanian passport, which he never scrutinised – luckily he only looked at the title page and didn't examine the expiry date.

I started working double shifts at the Naked Turtle, to save money, and at the same time I met two people who were to become very close

---

[2] See Michael Davis (2008), *Street Gang: The Complete History of Sesame Street*, New York: Viking Penguin.
[3] Malcolm Gladwell (2000), *The Tipping Point: How Little Things Can Make a Big Difference*, New York: Little, Brown and Company.

friends. Their friendship, company and inquisitiveness invariably made me work harder on my English. At the same time I was also spending a considerable amount of time in the company of new and challenging books and ideas, as well as taking numerous illegal substances.

Both of them were about my age. Caroline Fathering was my first ever friend in London. She'd previously worked at the Naked Turtle, so would come and sit at the bar and chat with old friends. She was going out with a Lebanese guy and she and I hit it off straight away. At the time she was looking for somewhere to live and I asked Salah if she could stay with us. He agreed. Caroline was just a friend, not a lover.

How would I describe her? She'd endured a fractious relationship with her mother, and her father had died in tragic circumstances. Despite this, she was a positive person and emotionally strong. She was 'middle-class' and her ambition was to travel, write and paint. Often we would discuss spiritual books and ideas together, sometimes late into the night.

Stephen Torsi also worked at the Naked Turtle, at the same time as I did. And we also lived together for a while. Once a year, at Christmas, he'd go home to see his parents in Southport, Merseyside, and I'd go with him. In due course, his parents, Denise and Toni, became like my adoptive parents. I was the first Arab they'd ever met. Toni was a chef and Denise worked in the theatre.

*

Caroline and Stephen introduced me to books and also to music, particularly bands like the Beatles. With Stephen particularly I could talk for hours. He had a vivid and fabulous imagination. Both of them helped me improve my understanding of the history of ideas and philosophy, and helped develop what I might call my creative imagination.

An early 'turning point' in my life came when they both enthusiastically introduced me to Kahlil Gibran's short book, *The Prophet*.[4]

If Shakespeare is the best-selling poet of all time, and if Lao-tzu is second, then third is Kahlil Gibran, who owes his position to one book, *The Prophet*, a collection of 26 prose poems, delivered as sermons by a fictional wise man in a faraway time and place. Since its first publication, in 1923, it's sold more than nine million copies in its American edition alone. *The Prophet* has been recited at countless weddings and funerals. It's also quoted in books and articles on training art teachers, determining criminal responsibility, enduring ectopic pregnancy and sleep disorders, and even 'the news that your son is gay'.[5] Its words appear in advertisements for marriage counsellors, chiropractors, learning-disability specialists and face cream.

The book's journey – like its author's – wasn't easy. Gibran was often dismissed as being a less than average writer. Indeed, his own publisher, Alfred A. Knopf, was far from enthusiastic. When asked, in 1965, who the audience for *The Prophet* was, Knopf replied that he had no idea. 'It must be a cult,' he said, a somewhat ungrateful response from the man to whom *The Prophet* had been a cash cow for more than forty years.[6]

---

[4]This section relies heavily on Joan Acocella's succinct article, 'The Prophet Motive', first published in *The New Yorker*, 7 January 2008.
[5]*Ibid.*
[6]*Ibid.*

Kahlil Gibran was born in 1883, in Lebanon, in the village of
Bsharri. At that time, Lebanon was part of Syria, which in turn
was part of the Ottoman Empire. Gibran, by his biographer Robin
Waterfield's account, was a 'brooding and soulful child'.[7] Gibran later
moved to Boston and New York, where he wrote under the patronage
of Mary Haskell, the headmistress of a girls' school. He began to
write in English and with the third of his English-language books,
The Prophet, he hit the proverbial jackpot. So what exactly made this
small and unusual book so fantastically successful and made it strike
such a chord with me?

It was perhaps the first example I'd ever encountered, ever read, of
what has come to be called a 'life lesson' book. This small book taught
me some lessons as to how to live my life and gave me insight into
how, perhaps, the mind, human relationships and the world work. Let
me elaborate.

At the opening of the book, we are told that Almustafa, a holy
man, has been living in exile for 12 years, in a city called Orphalese.[8]
A ship comes to take him back to the island of his birth. Saddened
by his departure, people gather around and ask him for his final
words of wisdom. He willingly obliges, and his writings, sermons or
musings occupy most of the book. Almustafa's advice is apt, useful:
love involves suffering; children should be given their independence.
Who, these days, would say otherwise?

More than the soundness of its advice, however, the mere fact that
The Prophet was a life lesson book – or, more precisely, 'inspirational

---

[7]Robin Waterfield (1998), *Prophet: The Life and Times of Kahlil Gibran*, London: Allen Lane.
[8]As Acocella, *op. cit.*, points out: When *The Prophet* was published, Gibran himself had been
living in New York, in 'exile' from Lebanon, also for 12 years.

literature'[9] – probably ensured a substantial readership from the very start. Gibran's closest modern counterpart is the Brazilian Paulo Coelho, whose books have sold over seventy million copies and whom I'll discuss later.

The most obvious influences on *The Prophet* are, of course, the teachings of Jesus and also the German philosopher Friedrich Nietzsche, especially his *Thus Spake Zarathustra*. There are enormous points of comparison between Nietzsche and Gibran, the main one being the similarity between the two prophets, Zarathustra and Almustafa. In his short examination of Gibran's work, Suheil Bushrui explores the comparison:

> Both are strangers among men who give of their wisdom and then retire to their distant island homes. But their respective teachings differ enormously in substance; whereas Zarathustra preaches a destructive code of self and self-reliance, Almustafa's message to the people of Orphalese is a passionate belief in the healing power of universal love and the unity of being, based on the mystic traditions of the Sufis.[10]

Bushrui recounts that Almustafa first speaks about 'love' and argues that this is the 'most beautiful of all his sermons', in which he states that love is:

> ...to know the pain of too much tenderness. To be wounded by your own understanding of love; and to bleed willingly and joyfully.

---

[9]Acocella, *op. cit.*
[10]Suheil Bushrui (1987), *Kahlil Gibran of Lebanon*, Gerrards Cross: Colin Smythe, p. 68.

To wake at dawn with a winged heart and give thanks for another day of loving…[11]

This concept of love as wounding and painful, even while it can 'lift to ecstasy',[12] is found in the writings of both Sufis and also the medieval Christian mystics. Almustafa's insistence on the essential identity of love, joy, pain and sorrow, is a major feature of the book.

Indeed, the book does sound religious, which, in a way, it is. Gibran was familiar with both Buddhist and Muslim holy books, and above all with the Bible, in both its Arabic and King James translations. In *The Prophet* he integrated many seemingly diverse influences and traditions and presented his work in a seamless manner perfect for those readers, 'many of whom longed for the comforts of religion but did not wish to pledge allegiance to any church, let alone to any deity who might have left a record of how he wanted them to behave'.[13]

Sadly, for Gibran's sense of self-worth, he was not a success with Manhattan's 'better class of artists'. He seldom turns up in any literary memoirs of the period. Indeed, perhaps the only mention he receives is in Edmund Wilson's journal of the 1920s, who says that 'Gibran the Persian' was at a dinner party that a friend of his attended.[14]

I remember first reading the book, carefully and repeatedly, and some of Gibran's poems, musings and thoughts have remained with me. Indeed they've helped shape my life. Consider his thoughts on children:

---

[11]Kahlil Gibran (1924), *The Prophet*, New York: Alfred A. Knopf, p. 13.
[12]Bushrui (1987), p. 70.
[13]Acocella, *op. cit.*
[14]*Ibid.*

Your children are not your children. They are the sons and daughters of Life's longing for itself. They come through you but not from you, And though they are with you yet they belong not to you… You are the bows from which your children as living arrows are sent forth.[15]

I've always thought this gentle reminder as to the independence of children is wise and helpful, as are Gibran's thoughts on joy and sorrow:

Your joy is your sorrow unmasked. And the selfsame well from which your laughter rises was oftentimes filled with your tears… Is not the cup that holds your wine the very cup that was burned in the potter's oven?[16]

Remember, I'd received no philosophical or religious education of any merit when growing up in either Kuwait or Jordan. A book like Gibran's was like being struck by a thunderbolt. I was also dipping into all sorts of other books at the time – for example, I was reading religious encyclopedias, books on ancient history, all forms of literature – and Gibran's ideas always reminded me of that Jain notion of 'equanimity' – treating success and failure in the same way, becoming neither overly attached nor overly averse to anything.

I remember that one of Caroline's favourite Gibran sayings concerned death, where he says, 'When you have reached the mountaintop, then you shall begin to climb. And when the earth shall claim your limbs, then shall you truly dance.'[17]

---

[15]Kahlil Gibran (2013 edition), *The Prophet*, London: Vintage Books, pp. 19–20.
[16]*Ibid.*, p. 34.
[17]*Ibid.*, p. 99.

Gibran's coffin rests in a deconsecrated monastery, Mar Sarkis, in Bsharri, which he chose for that purpose. Robin Waterfield, his biographer, has visited it. He says that he found a crack in the cover of the casket and that, when he looked into it, he saw straight through to the back as if the body had disappeared. This seems a fitting, if sad, conclusion.[18]

It is, of course, not my place to judge my own life. I may have lived a life as contradictory or as morally ambiguous as Gibran's. But I can honestly and earnestly claim that much of what I have achieved or endeavoured to achieve has been motivated and created through what I learned from this little book. Gibran taught me that there were always (at least) two sides to the same story, and two ways of looking at something.

*

I think that both Stephen and Caroline could see that I was starting way behind them, in terms of philosophy in general and inspirational life-lesson literature in particular. They patiently explained things to me and gently increased my intake. One of the next books on their list was *Tuesdays with Morrie*.[19] In it, newspaper sports columnist Mitch Albom recounts the time he spent with his 78-year-old sociology professor at Brandeis University, Morrie Schwartz, who was dying from amyotrophic lateral sclerosis (ALS). The name Morrie comes from its meaning in Hebrew (*mori* ירום), which translates as 'my teacher'.

---

[18]Acocella, *op. cit.*

[19]*Tuesdays with Morrie*, first published by Sphere, topped the *New York Times* non-fiction bestsellers of 2000. The hardcover, paperback and audio versions have sold some 16 million copies worldwide and have been translated into 45 languages, from Bengali to Burmese and Hindi to Malay.

Albom was a successful sports columnist for the *Detroit Free Press*, despite his childhood dream of being a pianist. After seeing him on *Nightline*, Albom called Schwartz, who remembered his former pupil despite the lapse of 16 years. Albom was prompted to travel from Michigan to Massachusetts to visit Schwartz, which he continued to do on a regular basis, and the resulting book is based on these fourteen Tuesday meetings, supplemented with Schwartz's lectures and life experiences.

Their conversations cover all sorts of themes and topics, including acceptance, communication, love, values, openness and happiness. Albom emphasises the importance of forging a culture of one's own to transcend the tyranny of popular culture, arguing that the media is predominantly negative and preoccupied with death, hatred, violence and depression.

'The truth is...once you learn how to die, you learn how to live.' This is what Morrie says on the fourth Tuesday in response to Mitch's question about how one can prepare for death. He responds with a Buddhist philosophy that every day, one must ask the bird on his shoulder if that day is the day he will die. The philosophy serves as a metaphor for his awareness that his death may come at any moment. Morrie hopes that Mitch will realise that this bird is on everyone's shoulder at every moment of his or her lives, despite how young or old they may be. When he tells Mitch that one must know how to die before one can know how to live, he means that one must accept the possibility of one's own death before he can truly appreciate what he has on earth, as the sobering awareness of it all being out of reach one day prompts the urge to appreciate and value what one can have only for a limited period of time, and to use every moment of that time doing something that one will not regret when the bird sings its last note.

This particular book made me weep with joy. It spoke to an inner awareness that life had to be lived to the full, that I had to create my own life, my own culture, live my life in the way that I – and only I – saw fit and not try and live someone else's life or live by someone else's rules. I began to see life in terms of choices and pathways.

*

Besides reading, the other aspect of my life heavily influenced by Stephen concerned so-called 'illegal drug use'.

The first time I ever took an 'e' (ecstasy tablet)[20] was with Stephen in East London, maybe Hackney, I can't exactly remember where we were. While I worked at the Naked Turtle restaurant I never ever drank any alcohol. However, I did use a number of illegal drugs. It is not something I condone, but at the time drugs were a big part of my life in London. I would use them to relax and enter, albeit briefly, another world.

*

Other than London, the only other place I ventured to – perhaps surprisingly, some might think– was the Bedfordshire town of Luton. I knew someone from Jordan who'd settled in Luton, so on days off work I'd drive there and spend time with him. The first car I bought cost about £200. It was a beaten-up and barely drivable Volvo. The first time I travelled from East Sheen to Luton took seven hours instead of the anticipated ninety minutes. The reason was that I went round

---

[20]Ecstasy (also known by its chemical name, MDMA [3,4-methylenedioxy-methamphetamine]) is often seen as the original designer drug because of its high-profile links to dance music culture in the late 1980s and early 1990s. Clubbers took ecstasy to feel energised and happy, and to stay awake and dance for hours.

and round and round the M25 in continuous circles. I remember stopping at a petrol station and, in a panic, asking an Indian guy for directions: 'I'm trying to get the directions to Luton, can you help me?' He smiled and replied, 'You asked me the very same question three hours ago.'

Through this old Jordanian contact I met someone called Mazen, an Iraqi refugee, who was Shia. I, of course, was Sunni, but it made no difference to our relationship as Muslims and friends.

In 1997 I left the Naked Turtle and made Luton my temporary home. I was living my life in a completely different way to what I'd experienced in East Sheen. Frankly, it felt like living in Islamabad. To begin with, there were over 300 mosques, all working as separate businesses, and all following different Islamic traditions or sects. I thought it was a ridiculous town.

I found a job, at Marcello's, an Italian trattoria in the nearby market town of Hitchin. Marcello's, on the delightfully pretty and rustic Sun Street, served various types of Italian food such as antipasto, ravioli, carbonara, bruschetta, minestrone, marinara, tagliatelli and tiramisu, and as a result of working there my basic culinary skills improved. I worked for an amazing boss. While there I also met two wonderful women, Haley and Nadine. Nadine was older than me and remains an important part of my life. She was married, very wealthy, lived in a large country house and didn't get on particularly well with her husband. While Haley helped me with my English, Nadine helped me with my life. She helped me understand gender differences, the rules of relationships, the rules of the game. She was always a great support to me, in every aspect of my life.

*

Mazen was an Iraqi refugee. As I mentioned, in one sense Luton shocked me, although at times it was agreeable because I felt like I was living in a Muslim country. There were mosques everywhere and all the shops were halal, so I didn't feel like I was actually in the UK. In Luton I lived in a big house, paying rent, and Mazen's brother had a large garage nearby where Mazen himself worked.

On Sundays, I would play football with some guys, one of whom, I later discovered, was related to one of the 7/7 bombers.[21] There were always lots of young Muslim guys in the street, talking intensely and preaching. Some were members of the Hizb ut-Tahrir party, a pan-Islamic political organisation,[22] which is commonly associated with the goal of all Muslim countries unifying as an Islamic state or caliphate ruled by Islamic law (*sharia*), and with a *caliph* or head of state elected by Muslims. Following the 7 July 2005 London bombings the British government announced its intention to ban the party, but then abandoned its plans. According to the *Independent*, Prime Minister Blair 'shelved the ban after warnings from police, intelligence chiefs, and civil liberties groups that it is a non-violent group, and driving it underground could backfire'.[23]

In July 2007, the then Leader of the Opposition, David Cameron, asked the new Prime Minister, Gordon Brown, why the organisation hadn't been banned, arguing it was an extremist group. Brown responded that more evidence would be needed before banning

---

[21]The 7 July 2005 London bombings (often referred to as '7/7') were a series of coordinated suicide bomb attacks in central London which targeted civilians using the public transport system during the morning rush hour.

[22]See Sadek Hamid (2007), 'Islamic Political Radicalism in Britain: the case of Hizb-ut-Tahrir', in Tahir Abbas (2007), *Islamic Political Radicalism: A European Perspective*, Edinburgh: Edinburgh University Press, pp. 145–59.

[23]Nigel Morris, 'PM Forced to Shelve Islamist Group Ban', *Independent*, 18 July 2006.

a group and, when pressed further, John Reid, the previous Home Secretary, stepped in, arguing that there had already been two reviews of the group with insufficient evidence to justify a ban.

The members and spokesmen of Hizb ut-Tahrir were highly eloquent, and were regarded as one of the 'lesser evils'. In Luton I also encountered numerous *Wahhabis* (ultraconservative orthodox Sunni Muslims). On a Sunday they would stand in the town centre and shout, 'Kill, kill, kill the infidels!' Now that did shock me. They were talking about maiming and murdering people such as my best friends Caroline, Nadine and Stephen. I thought, 'Why isn't the government doing something about these people?'

Some of the Luton mosques were supported by Saudis, others by Emiratis, Qataris or Pakistanis; some mosques were Sunni, others Shia. Businesses would support particular mosques. It's important to note that *inside* the mosques the teaching I listened to was conventional and totally acceptable. But outside it was a different story. To their credit, the mosques refused to let the proselytising and irresponsible speakers inside to preach.

I knew quite a few Pakistani girls in Luton, educated and born in the UK and then forced to marry cousins in some far-off Pakistani village. The narrative is as follows: the husband comes to the UK, doesn't speak English, becomes a taxi driver, then the father-in-law supports him and helps him buy a house. Then the husband and wife have any number of problems, and divorce. With his newly acquired passport, the husband will return to Pakistan, marry again, have lots of kids and bring them all back to the UK.

Personally, I've never taken any government money in the form of income support or other benefits. But I never failed to notice the

Luton dole queue and the crowded and dreary post offices on Monday mornings. Inside they were full of young guys, the taxis they drove parked outside with engines idling, guys who had a nice new car at home and holidays booked every year.

*

In 1998, and on the spur of the moment, I decided to take a holiday to Scotland. In particular, I wanted to go to Edinburgh. It had all began with a trip to see the film *Braveheart*, where I loved Mel Gibson in the leading role, but in terms of my knowledge of the country, that's as far as it went. Edinburgh was wholly different from London or Luton, and I would come to cherish the city as my home.

3

Edinburgh

A good traveller has no fixed plans, and is not intent on arriving.
LAO TZU

If London was an alien city, Edinburgh was another planet.
JESS WALTER

There are two seasons in Scotland. June and winter.
BILLY CONNOLLY

I skipped as I left the cinema after watching the Mel Gibson film for the first time, and was highly emotional. What a story! Soon afterwards I read up on the film, the background and some Scottish history.

In 1280, King Edward Longshanks, played by Patrick McGoohan of *Danger Man* and *The Prisoner* fame, invades and conquers Scotland following the death of Alexander III, who leaves no heir to the throne. Young William Wallace, played heroically by Mel Gibson, witnesses Longshanks' treachery, survives the deaths of his father and brother, and is taken abroad to Rome by his paternal uncle Argyle, where he's educated. Years later, Longshanks grants his noblemen some privileges in Scotland, including *jus primae noctis* (or *droit du seigneur*, the right of the lord to have sex with female subjects on their wedding nights). When Wallace returns home, he reunites with his childhood friend, Hamish, and also falls in love with his other childhood friend, Murron MacClannough, played by the delectable Catherine McCormack. They marry in secret, so she won't be obliged to spend the night with the local English lord. Wallace rescues her from being raped by English soldiers, but she's captured and publicly executed. In retribution, Wallace and his clan slaughter the English garrison.

As Wallace's legend spreads, hundreds of Scots from the surrounding clans join him. He leads his army to victory at Stirling and then kills Longshanks' nephew, sending his head back. Worried by the threat of the rebellion, Longshanks sends his son's wife, Isabella of France, to try to negotiate with Wallace, hoping Wallace will kill her and as a result make the French king declare war. Wallace, of course, refuses the bribe sent with Isabella by Longshanks, but Isabella falls for Wallace. Longshanks prepares an army to invade Scotland.

Warned by Isabella of the coming invasion, Wallace implores the Scottish nobility that immediate action is needed. Leading the English army himself, Longshanks confronts the Scots at Falkirk and the Scots lose the battle. Wallace wages a guerrilla war against the English for the next seven years, assisted by Isabella, with whom he eventually has an affair. Isabella exacts revenge on the now terminally ill Longshanks by telling him she's pregnant with Wallace's child, and is intent on ending Longshanks' line.

In London, Wallace is brought before an English magistrate, tried for high treason, and condemned to public torture and beheading. Even while being hung, drawn and quartered, Wallace refuses to submit to the king. Wallace shouts, 'Freedom!' and the judge immediately orders his death.

In 1314, Robert the Bruce,[1] now Scotland's king, leads a Scottish army before a ceremonial line of English troops on the fields of Bannockburn, where he is to formally accept English rule. As he begins to ride towards the English, he invokes Wallace's memory, imploring his men to fight with him as they did with Wallace. Robert then leads his army into battle against the stunned English, winning the Scots their freedom.

Along with a friend, I left the cinema, having shed some tears. We cheered all the way home. I immediately wanted to visit Scotland.

*

So, I was attuned to liking the country, but when I actually visited, I fell in love with her. I'd read about a four-day scuba-diving course in Oban and, without any research or hesitation, I joined. To get to Oban I first took the train to Edinburgh. I walked along a busy and friendly Princes Street, saw the gardens and the castle and thought, 'Wow!' It was so different to Luton, to Putney, to anywhere I'd ever been.

The course in Oban was amazing, despite the fact that underwater I couldn't actually see anything and it was continuously cold and miserable. What I *do* remember is that I ate plenty of wonderful oysters.

I then returned to Edinburgh and truly fell in love with the city, even though I was staying in a small and poky B&B in Minto Street. I was still working at Marcello's in Hitchin, but I knew I had to make Edinburgh my home, and so I started looking for a flat, or even a

---

[1]See G. W. S. Barrow (1998), *Robert Bruce and the Community of the Realm of Scotland*, Edinburgh: Edinburgh University Press.

room in a shared house. After a day or so I found a basement flat near the B&B, also in Minto Street, in the Newington district of the city.

Newington is about a fifteen-minute walk south of the city centre, namely the Royal Mile and Princes Street. It has an interesting history. It's the easternmost district of the area formerly covered by the Burgh Muir, gifted to the city by David I in the twelfth century. Even after the 1586 consolidation of land rights over the Burgh Muir, the area remained largely rural. The Newington Estate was purchased sometime before 1672 by John Lauder, a Baillie and Treasurer of Edinburgh, who thereafter took the landed designation 'of Newington', until he became Sir John Lauder, 1st Baronet of Fountainhall.

I was absolutely obsessed with Edinburgh and her history, and so read everything I could get my hands on, discovering more and more interesting facts about the city. When the South Bridge was built in 1788, parts of Newington became available for development and migration there commenced, generally into small villas. Many of these can still be seen. Many of the tenement buildings, however, didn't emerge for another hundred years. Then, as now, students heavily populated Newington.

*

I returned to Marcello's and told my boss, who I really liked, that I intended to leave within the month. I explained the reason – 'I love Scotland' – and although bemused, he wished me good luck. And so, exactly one month after my first visit, I left southern England for Scotland.

At that time I didn't know a single soul in Scotland. But it didn't matter, because I was so in love with the city – the festival, the castle, the gardens, university buildings, even the weather and the dark skies, the whole romance of it all.

The Minto Street flat I had moved into was cold and I heated it with a system operated by an electric meter that regularly swallowed numerous coins. But it was my flat. Soon after moving in, I rented a piano – because, strange as it might seem, I'd always wanted to play Beethoven's *Moonlight Sonata*. I didn't want to actually learn the music; I just wanted to learn how to play that piece. So, one morning when I was walking along Nicholson Street, I saw a music shop, with pianos and other instruments in the window. After some haggling with the friendly and amused proprietor, I rented a piano for £300 for a period of six months. The guy in the shop gave me the name of a teacher, who I called and arranged to meet. When we met later, I said to her, 'I want to play the *Moonlight Sonata*, Vivaldi's *Four Seasons*, and some pieces by Mozart.' She appeared surprised and understandably asked me, 'Don't you want to learn the music?' And I said, 'No, I just want to be able to play the pieces.'

About six months down the line I was able to do so. It took two lessons a week to get me to that stage, and it wasn't easy, so I was proud of myself and my determination to succeed. I did reflect at the time that one of the 'qualities' I possessed was a determination to set myself precise tasks or goals and ensure that I reach them. Once I'd started on that piano nothing was going to stop me from successfully playing Beethoven.

*

At the time I was learning the piano pieces, I was going out with a quite crazy woman called Tracy, who I'd first met when I simply went into a shop to buy a mobile phone. She took a lot of drugs. All sorts, in fact everything but heroin. She would inject, but not with heroin. I thought I loved her. We had such happy and wild and interesting times together. I went to the T in the Park festival with her for the first time, and saw the incredible Massive Attack and also Basement Jaxx. But, after a few months, and to use the common parlance of the time, I had to finish the relationship because she was 'doing my head in'. Her emotional neediness and her reckless behaviour began to take its toll on me and, besides, I was a little scared that I might copy her excessive drug-taking. But the emotional fallout that was involved had a positive consequence: I realised I wanted to get serious with my life and continue the education I'd half-heartedly begun in Jordan.

*

I still had a little money left – despite the costs involved in supporting Tracy's habitual drug use – so I decided to take another short course, this time in 'aerobics instruction'. At the time I was completely unfit, a little overweight, grey in the face with black rings beneath my eyes, taking no real exercise and occasionally still relying on marijuana. But through attending the course I began to meet some new drug-free people, which was quite refreshing. Then, soon afterwards, I decided I wanted to try and somehow complete the hospitality training I had begun in Amman, so I started looking around at universities and various possibilities that, at first glance, looked unlikely.

However, I soon found what I was looking for at Queen Margaret College, an Edinburgh institution with a quite venerable past. It was founded in 1875, as The Edinburgh School of Cookery and Domestic

Economy, by Christian Guthrie Wright and Louisa Stevenson,[2] both members of the Edinburgh Ladies' Educational Association. It was originally a women-only institution, with the twin aims of improving women's access to higher education and improving the diets of working-class families. Teaching was initially delivered via lectures at the Royal Museum, supplemented by a programme of public lectures and demonstrations delivered nationwide, but in 1877 the school established a base in Haymarket. The school moved in 1891 to Atholl Crescent, expanding its courses and offering residential places, and later, in 1909, it was brought under the public control of the Scottish Education Department and is now called Queen Margaret University.

Despite my growing fantasy of enrolling at this venerable institution and imagining a career in catering or hotel management, I faced the problem of my illegal status. I was an alien. How would I possibly get into such a prestigious British institution?

In the past, when faced with such issues, I'd always feigned ignorance concerning various pieces of documentation or 'papers', or I would endlessly prevaricate, or cite the loss of such documentation. The truth was I had nothing. In fact, as an example, I didn't even have a driving licence. I painfully remember the time I appeared at a UK magistrate's court on a speeding charge, after I stupidly drove at over 140 mph. The unimpressed magistrate said I would receive six points on my licence. I recall thinking to myself, 'And where on earth are you gonna put the six points?' Afterwards I never responded to any letters I received about the points or the licence.

[2]See Tom Begg, (2004), 'Cour, Ethel Maud De la (1869–1957)', *Oxford Dictionary of National Biography*, Oxford: OUP.

So, despite the issue of my alien status nagging away at me, I made some initial enquiries at Queen Margaret College. With no substantive or relevant paperwork to present to them, all I had was what was sent from Jordan. I'd previously asked my dad to send me the certificates from my high school in Kuwait and also from Ammon College in Amman.

One late, drizzly Friday afternoon, I met with the admissions officer, a nice young woman who, after my reasonably successful attempt at flirting, told me she thought I had 'beautiful eyes'. I said I'd misplaced my documents and had no ID, although I did have a National Insurance number. I was facing a critical situation: as a home student the fees were minimal, but as an international overseas student the fees were something like £12,000. After a somewhat meandering conversation lasting well over an hour, I was, amazingly and bizarrely, offered a place as a home student. I have no idea how it happened. I'd said to her that I didn't have my passport with me but that I could bring it in if necessary. Instead, I simply gave her my National Insurance number as proof of identity, and showed her a provisional driving licence. She then assumed, I guess, that I was a domestic student.

That young admissions officer's decision did not completely change my life – only I could do that – but, nonetheless, her decision certainly took me down a new path which would have important consequences.

I'd lied to the admissions officer and that was wrong. However, at the time I looked at it in the following way: I wasn't directly hurting anyone in particular, I wasn't really scamming anyone. I just wanted to continue to design my life my way and I really, really wanted to study and learn, and then give something back in return: contribute to the

Edinburgh economy and to Scotland, the country I was increasingly calling 'home'.

*

After a mere three months on the Hotel Management and Hospitality course, I was moved up to the second year, primarily because I was competent and experienced. My tutor had noticed this, especially in the various pieces of practical work we undertook in the kitchen and at the tables. At the beginning of the course I was made to sit two short entrance tests and I surprised even myself when I passed. However, it was evident to me and everyone else that my English language skills, both orally and written, were still a 'work in progress'. Many of my fellow students, especially Lindsay, Ruth, Christine and Hayley, helped me with essays and other written assignments. We became good friends and helped each other as much as we could. My tutor was also helpful and understanding, as he knew I was genuinely passionate about the hospitality industry. Most of the other students on the course wanted to be hotel managers, but I wanted to be a general manager – my ambition was for the top job; I was aiming to be the head honcho.

While I was at Queen Margaret's I worked two jobs, putting in many hours at both of them. One was at a health club called Next Generation. The other, more significant one was at a restaurant called the Buffalo Grill, in Stockbridge. There I met Mark Porter, who both proverbially opened the doors of Edinburgh to me and also became my best and closest friend.

The Buffalo Grill was always busy. There were three sittings per night and diners were given about one and a half hours to eat, so there was never enough time for anyone to enjoy a relaxed and lengthy dinner. Buffalo Grill was a 'steak and chips' restaurant, as compared with the 'fine dining' of Marcello's. I waited tables at the Buffalo Grill and fitted in just fine.

I met a woman called Denise when I did an aerobics instructor course in Wester Hill, a slightly rough and down-at-heel area of Edinburgh. Soon afterwards, Denise and I looked for a flat together, just as friends. It might sound somewhat insignificant, but this move was highly symbolic for me, because I was now living on the first floor, no longer deep down in the basement! There were five of us, sharing a huge flat in the centre of the city, with the gardens and the castle in sight. It was great. At about the same time I also did a bronze medal qualification in lifesaving, and subsequently worked as a lifeguard. I bought a Mercedes from Mazen, my Luton friend, and finally got rid of the Honda.

Mark Porter, from the Buffalo Grill, was central to the next phase of my life, a crucial and transformative time when I became a habitual user of the party drug ecstasy. At the same time that this heady nocturnal life was unfolding, I got my first real job, at Edinburgh's prestigious Sheraton Hotel. I started in banqueting and – running ahead of the narrative – then moved on to become head of room service, and finally assistant head of food and beverages. I loved working at the Sheraton. It eventually became more of a managerial role and so I wore an Armani suit. I was learning so much and I was really confident with customers. If my life hadn't taken the turn it eventually did, I'd have been a general manager somewhere in the Middle East, somewhere like Medina or Makkah, at a nice hotel, speaking to customers and fellow staff in Arabic and English and married to an Arab wife.

*

My life as a clubber only took off after meeting Mark, who like me was interested in finding pleasure in new places. Our primary and favoured destination was an Edinburgh club called Taste, which featured local DJ legends Fisher & Price, and was an Edinburgh institution after running for 16 years, one of the capital's most-loved, gay-friendly, open-minded club nights. Its tag line was 'For Perverts and Extraverts', but as a matter of fact it was 50/50 gay and straight, and seemed absolutely normal to me. I never felt uneasy there, and there was never any trouble – probably because although there was booze on the premises, we all drank water. Through our nights at Taste, I met people I'd never have met elsewhere, and mainly from two separate camps: so-called 'respectable' people like teachers, social workers, nurses, bankers, health visitors, shop girls, academics, insurance agents, policemen and tax inspectors, and, on the other hand, bodyguards, low-level criminals, tattoo artists, taxi drivers, dealers and all sorts of clubbers.

Through ecstasy, Mark and I opened up to each other, and I shared my life and thoughts and emotions in a way that I never previously had. We talked about anything and everything. There was a core group of about ten of us, although on certain occasions this could expand to twenty.

Taste was strictly Sunday nights only. As Mark and I, and some of our joint friends, were in the hospitality industry, we worked Saturdays, and so Sundays and Mondays were our days off. We could, if you like, get a clear run at it. We'd often join people halfway through *their* Saturday night and then just continue onwards and upwards. We knew all the faces, week in, week out. It was always full to the rafters, like a small sweatbox. It was home to the weird and the wonderful.

There were men with waxed moustaches who would prance about and then lurk around, and others who would wear outrageous outfits, like a couple of regulars who dressed as a pair of golden mermaids. There were never any drug raids, despite the actual presence of drugs – perhaps because there was never any trouble.

Clubbing was a huge part of my life. I loved to move, gyrate, dance, and I loved the feeling of happiness and 'love', and the effect that drugs had on my mind. It was the shared experience as much as anything else: the shared experience of taking drugs in a particular place with valued friends, which ultimately led to long-standing friendships; I recall someone saying the same about the Hacienda[3] experience in Manchester. Like those Mancunians, every weekend we would dance, have a giggle and take a pill, rather than getting blotto and starting a fight.

I managed to keep working during this clubbing phase. I would go to Taste, then go to someone's house until eight in the morning, and then be ready for work at ten, at which point I'd work a full day, go home and sleep. At Ramadan I would stop all of this, go to a mosque and stay there quietly for a few days. I'd read the *Qur'an* and 'cleanse' myself.

But drugs did open my mind. I'm not advocating drugs for anyone else, and I've seen many victims of various types of drug use; I'm just saying that at that time in my life ecstasy in particular opened and sharpened my imagination.

*

Ecstasy is controversially used in therapy to open people's minds. There's a lot of anecdotal – as well as some often contradictory scientific – evidence as to the effects of the drug.

---

[3]For a history see Tony Wilson (2002), *24 Hour Party People*, London: Pan MacMillan.

All I can say, as a user but not a scientist, is that I experienced joy and euphoria using ecstasy, perhaps even 'love', although I won't make that claim. Equally, without doubt, I never experienced any adverse or negative effects from using this illegal substance and found the ecstasy environment preferable to the majority of Edinburgh pubs. Drugs also allowed me to talk about different emotions.

It was either Mark, or another friend – perhaps Cameron or Ross – who introduced me to a book on the philosophy of psychedelic drug use, which further opened my mind. Although I had little interest in LSD or other hallucinatory drugs, I had used them and was as interested in their effects as I was in those of ecstasy.

Aldous Huxley's *The Doors of Perception*,[4] published in 1954, describes and debates his own use of the cactus-derived drug mescaline. Later, in 1965, it influenced Jim Morrison to name his band The Doors, and it remains controversial. It takes the form of Huxley's recollection of a mescaline trip that took place one afternoon, and takes its title from a phrase in William Blake's 1793 poem *The Marriage of Heaven and Hell*. In the book, Huxley recalls the insights he experienced, which range from the purely aesthetic to what he describes as 'sacramental vision'.

Back in the 1930s Huxley had been interested in spirituality and had used so-called alternative therapies for some time. In the late 1930s he had become interested in the spiritual teaching of Vedanta and in 1945 he published *The Perennial Philosophy*, which set out a philosophy that he believed was found among mystics of all religions.[5]

---

[4] Aldous Huxley (1954), *The Doors of Perception*, London: Chatto and Windus.
[5] Aldous Huxley (1946 edition), *The Perennial Philosophy*, London: Chatto and Windus.

He'd known for some time of visionary experiences achieved by taking drugs in certain non-Christian religions.

Huxley first became aware of mescaline after reading an academic paper written by Humphry Osmond, a British psychiatrist working at the Weyburn Mental Hospital, Saskatchewan, in early 1952. Osmond's paper set out results from his research into schizophrenia using mescaline, and after reading it, Huxley sent Osmond a letter, putting himself forward as an experimental subject.

Osmond agreed to the suggestion and accordingly arrived at Huxley's house in West Hollywood on 3 May 1953. He had misgivings about giving the drug to Huxley, and wrote that he didn't 'relish the possibility, however remote, of being the man who drove Aldous Huxley mad', but instead found him an ideal subject.[6] In total, the experience lasted something like eight hours.

It took Huxley a month to write the book. He recalls that he was given four tenths of a gram at 11:00 a.m. one day in May 1953, and later experienced a great change in his perception of the external world. For example, he writes that by 12:30 p.m. a vase of flowers became the 'miracle, moment by moment, of naked existence'.

When he was in the garden, chairs took on such an immense intensity that he feared being overwhelmed. It gave him an insight into madness. He speculates that schizophrenia is the inability to escape from this reality into the world of common sense, and thus help would be essential.[7]

---

[6] See Sybille Bedford (1974), *Aldous Huxley: A Biography, Volume Two: 1939–1963*, London: Chatto & Windus, p. 144.
[7] See Huxley (1954), pp. 46–48.

The book finishes with Huxley's final reflections on the meaning of his experience. Firstly, he suggests that the urge to transcend one's self is universal through all times and cultures, and he suggests that better, healthier 'doors' are needed than alcohol and tobacco. He adds that mescaline has the advantage of not provoking violence in takers, but its effects last an inconveniently long time and some users can have negative reactions. Ideally, self-transcendence would be found in religion, but Huxley feels that it is unlikely that this will ever happen. However, he concludes that the person who has this experience will be transformed for the better.

Not all critics were kind to the book. Thomas Mann believed it demonstrated Huxley's escapism. He thought that while escapism found in mysticism might be honourable, drugs weren't, and concluded that the book was irresponsible, if not quite immoral, and would encourage young people to try mescaline.[8]

In October 1955, Huxley had an experience while on LSD that he considered more profound than those detailed in *The Doors of Perception*. He was overwhelmed to the point where he decided the previous experiments, described in that book, had been nothing but 'entertaining sideshows'. In a letter to Humphry Osmond, Huxley said that he'd experienced

...the direct, total awareness, from the inside, so to say, of Love as the primary and fundamental cosmic fact... I was this fact; or

---

[8] See Conrad Watt (1997) *Aldous Huxley*, pp. 394–395, London: RKP.

perhaps it would be more accurate to say that this fact occupied the place where I had been.[9]

*

No one outside of Edinburgh knew much about my life, my clubbing or my work at the Sheraton, nor my reflections on the meaning of life and the meaning of *my* life, and what I should do with it.

I hadn't seen my parents for a long time and could only telephone them at certain times. I was still sending Dad £500 a month, as I did when I first moved to the UK, and my mum would tell me on the telephone that she 'missed me', as I tried my best to reassure her that I was well, fit and healthy.

In Edinburgh I was being precisely who I wanted to be. Yet I now felt I had opened my mind to other things, to something 'beyond', and it was at this moment that I realised I wanted to try and reacquaint myself with Allah. This was not a well-articulated realisation, but, rather, I knew a great change was taking place within me. It was a change that was to lead me to India.

---

[9]See 'Letter to Humphry Osmond, 24 October 1955', in Laura Achera Huxley (1969), *This Timeless Moment*, London: Chatto & Windus.

4

India

*Man cannot discover new oceans unless he has the courage
to lose sight of the shore.*

ARISTOPHANES

There is more to life than increasing its speed.

MAHATMA GANDHI

*People tend to want to study under famous teachers. Yet there are
always people not considered distinguished by the public who could
teach them as effectively.*

ABŪ ḤĀMID MUḤAMMAD IBN MUḤAMMAD AL-GHAZĀLĪ

In early 2001 I decided I had to travel to India, because my friend
Stephen had spoken about it so many times and perhaps had
surreptitiously put the idea in my head. First of all, though, I needed
to return to Jordan. This had to be done in such a way that I'd be
able to return to Edinburgh whenever I wished. With this in mind, I
remembered a family friend from Amman, called Ammar. He was the
manager and coach of Jordan's taekwondo team and I explained my
problem. As luck would have it, Ammar was looking for a translator

for the team. He offered me the job, which I gratefully accepted and which secured my visa for a year.

So, with peace of mind concerning my future travel, I returned to Jordan. I stayed for about a month and then bought a ticket for India. My mum and dad knew nothing about the Western idea of 'the East' – the 'magical mystery tour', the hippie trail, or anything else of that sort of Indomania – so they were hardly understanding or sympathetic.

However, unlike my parents, my friend Stephen had read a lot about India, had travelled widely there, and talked with me and taught me a lot. It was through him that I learned all about the Beatles and their later brand of quasi-mystical music with Ravi Shankar, as well as George Harrison's interest in Bangladesh and Hare Krishna in particular, and Hinduism in general. My other close friend from the Naked Turtle days, Caroline, had also previously introduced me to a book that was central to the changes that were taking place in my life – Paulo Coelho's *The Alchemist* (Portuguese: *O Alquimista*). Caroline thought that I reminded her of the book's central character, Santiago. The book was another life-changer. I believe entirely in its message. I first read it in about 1997. To summarize what it meant to me: Allah knows my destiny but *I'm making it*. Allah knows the future, but Allah is not telling me how to live my life. The way I see it, Allah provides opportunities and puts people in my path, but everything depends on my *intention*, and my intention has always been to help my family and parents and brothers and sister, and to be kind and loving to those I encounter.

*

In 2014, Coelho's short novel reached its 303rd consecutive week on the *New York Times'* bestseller list. First published in 1988, and originally written in Portuguese by its Brazilian-born author, it has been translated into at least 67 languages and has sold well over 70 million copies.

An allegorical novel, *The Alchemist* follows the journey of a shepherd boy named Santiago. Born in a small town in Andalusia, he attends a seminary but longs to see the world. He finally summons the courage to ask his father for permission to become a shepherd so that he can travel through Andalusia. One night, in an abandoned church, he dreams of a child telling him that, if he travels to the Egyptian pyramids, he'll find a treasure.

Early into his journey he meets an old king, Melchizedek, who tells him to sell his sheep to travel to Egypt and introduces the idea of a Personal Legend (always capitalised in the book). One's Personal Legend 'is what you have always wanted to accomplish...[and]... everyone, when they are young, knows what their Personal Legend is.' Melchizedek is the king of Salem, a mysterious, far-off land, and appears to Santiago in the town square of Tarifa, where he tells him for the first time about the Soul of the World and his Personal Legend. While he appears at first to be wearing common Arab dress, at one point he pulls aside his cloak to reveal a gold breastplate encrusted with precious stones. Melchizedek adds that 'when you want something, all the universe conspires in helping you to achieve it'. This is the core theme of the book and something I firmly believe in.

Later, Santiago encounters the Alchemist of the book's title and is revealed to be his true disciple. The Alchemist dresses in black and uses a falcon to hunt for game, and is also in possession of the

Elixir of Life and the Philosopher's Stone. He says that people want to find only the treasure of their Personal Legend but not the Personal Legend itself. Santiago feels unsure about himself as he listens to the Alchemist's teachings: 'Those who don't understand their Personal Legend will fail to comprehend its teachings.'

It took Coelho a mere two weeks to write the book, and he has explained that he was able to write at this pace because the story was 'already written in [his] soul.'[1]

The Alchemist's main theme is about finding one's destiny, and it is more self-help or psychology than fiction. As I said earlier, Melchizedek tells Santiago, 'When you want something, all the universe conspires in helping you to achieve it.' My own life is absolutely based on this belief, which is why I rarely experience any fear or anxiety about whether or not I will successfully achieve any of my goals. His book is also a story of exploration, of adventure, and that too struck a chord.

Of course, the book is not without its critics. The central story of *The Alchemist* appears in previous works, including Rumi's story 'In Baghdad, Dreaming of Cairo: In Cairo, Dreaming of Baghdad,'[2] and a similar parable can also be found in a well-known Jewish chassidic story. Indeed, one of the chief criticisms of the book is that the story, praised for its fable-like simplicity, actually *is* a fable, a retelling of 'The Ruined Man Who Became Rich Again Through a Dream' (tale fourteen from the collection *One Thousand and One Nights*).[3]

---

[1] Interview with Hannah Pool (2009), *Guardian*, 19 March 2009, p. 9.
[2] See Mevlana Jalaluddin Rumi (ed. Kabir Helminski, 2000), *The Rumi Collection: An Anthology of Translations of Mevlana Jalaluddin Rumi*, San Francisco, CA: Shambhala Classics.
[3] See *Tales from the Thousand and One Nights [Arabian Nights]* (1973 edition, transl. N. J. Dawood), London: Penguin Classics.

Stephen and Caroline introduced me to numerous books, including another one which helped me formulate my thoughts and beliefs. *The Celestine Prophecy*, written by James Redfield and first published in 1993, is a novel that uses fiction to discuss various psychological and spiritual ideas rooted in ancient Eastern traditions and New Age spirituality. The main character undertakes a journey to find and understand a series of nine spiritual insights in an ancient manuscript in Peru.

According to one devotee of the book, the central message is simply about how we get and use energy. When we get enough energy, in the right ways, we can 'raise our vibration', and with a higher vibration we're better able to tap into our psychic and intuitive skills, and thus are better able to discover and live our true purpose in life.[4]

Redfield originally self-published *The Celestine Prophecy*, selling 100,000 copies out of the trunk of his Honda before Warner Books agreed to publish it.[5] He has admitted that, even though he considers the book to be a novel, his intention was to write a story in the shape of a parable, a story meant to illustrate a point.

The book makes absolute sense to me: increasingly we are beginning to understand more and more about our energy levels and the effects of physical health on the mind.

So, all of these books and conversations led me to some core beliefs about *my* destiny and the fact that, although Allah knows it, I create it. In the Middle East we all constantly speak of God's will. But it isn't. It's mine, my responsibility.

---

[4]See *The Skeptic's Dictionary* online.
[5]Press release, Llumina Press.

*

In April of 2002 I arrived to a fresh and mild spring in Delhi, and stayed for about 24 hours. Before I left Jordan, Stephen had enthused about Goa, but I knew I wasn't interested in that particular outpost of the hippie trail. I somehow intuitively knew that I wanted to get to Kashmir as soon as possible. So, after the one day in Delhi, which included a trip to the world-renowned Jama Masjid ('Friday' mosque), I headed off in a rickety bus all the way to Kashmir where, initially, I planned to stay two weeks but ended up staying for over six months. The journey from Delhi to Kashmir took over 48 hours, and the bus stopped every three hours or so. Young boys balancing pots on a yoke around their shoulders would bring on chai for us to buy, and then at other times we'd get off the tired bus and eat some roadside food, invariably lentil-based, and with fresh and spicy vegetables. The roads were small, often with rocks scattered across, and they slowly wound their way through the mountains.

When I first arrived in Kashmir, exhausted and somewhat disoriented, I spent far too long getting stoned. But soon afterwards I started getting out and about, meeting interesting people and, as a consequence, my drug use began to slow down.

At first I stayed on a houseboat on Nagin Lake, which acts like a mirror, with the beautiful snow-covered mountains reflected in the still water. On the more expensive boats moored alongside, houseboys would serve steaming cups of tea – sometimes English, and at other times Kashmiri, flavoured with cinnamon, cardamom and ginger. I'd sit quietly and watch exquisite sunsets, continuing to devour as many books as possible, and would occasionally venture out to eat cheap but delicious meals – Western, Kashmiri or Indian.

I shared the boat with a larger-than-life Norwegian former heroin addict, Trond. He was considerably older than me, his face was heavily lined, and he looked world-weary and worn out. Back in Norway, he'd held down an important and highly paid job in computing. His 'problem' had been excessive cocaine, and occasional heroin use. He was in Kashmir for rehab, funded partly by the Norwegian government and partly by himself. This rehabilitation took the form of people being nice to him, spending time and talking with him, and him receiving regular healthy food and exercise. It was a gentle process.

However, Trond also suffered from terrible mood swings and was, at times, difficult to be with. Nonetheless, we talked a lot about life, drugs and religion. We would visit travellers on other houseboats. Indeed, it was with Trond that I met Jews for the first time – mostly dope-smokers from north London, Golders Green, I think.

Trond's way of 'dealing with' not using heroin, or other opiates, was through 'cough medicine'. It was, I think, an Indian version or derivative of the famous Dr J. Collis Browne's Mixture. This 'mixture' was, itself, a version of his famous Chlorodyne, invented in the nineteenth century by John Collis Browne, a doctor in the British Indian Army. Its original therapeutic use was to treat cholera. Subsequently, Browne sold his formula to the pharmacist John Thistlewood Davenport, who advertised it widely as a treatment for cholera, diarrhoea, insomnia, neuralgia and migraines. As its principal ingredients were a mixture of laudanum (an alcoholic solution of opium), tincture of cannabis and chloroform, it readily lived up to its claims of relieving pain and acting as a sedative!

Trond would regularly leave the boat and buy up to 12 bottles of this cough medicine at any one time. It took me quite a while to realise that this medicine contained morphine, as he'd constantly go to great lengths to tell me he was 'clean'. To quench my thirst, I'd be drinking bottle after bottle of Coca-Cola while he drank his 'cough medicine'.

*

I got married to a Kashmiri village schoolteacher called Fatima. She was about 40 – no one appeared to know her exact date of birth, including her – and I was a mere 32. She spoke only a little English, and her attempts were worse than mine. But she was a loving and warm person. We organised a small 'wedding' ceremony, very basic but technically proper for someone in Kashmir. Fatima desperately wanted to have a child. I soon moved into her house with her extended family and stayed for two or three months. I wanted to continue to explore India and so told her, honestly and frankly, that if she became pregnant there would always be a reason for me to return to Kashmir. Sadly, she never got pregnant. We divorced and I've never seen her again.

*

In Kashmir I would go to the mosque every Friday, then soon afterwards it became a daily visit. This was also the time when I was beginning to develop an interest in Rumi, another figure who came to be influential in my life. I was soon aware of some of his wise and illuminating phrases:

The Way has been marked out. If you depart from it, you will perish. If you try to interfere with the signs on the road, you will be an evil-doer.

Life/Soul is like a clear mirror; the body is dust on it. Beauty in us is not perceived, for we are under the dust.

When we are dead, seek not our tomb in the earth, but find it in the hearts of men.[6]

Jalāl ad-Dīn Muhammad Rūmī, also known more popularly simply as Rūmī (1207–1273), was a thirteenth-century Persian poet, theologian and Sufi. His influence transcends national borders as well as ethnic divisions: Iranians, Tajiks, Turks, Greeks, Pashtuns, other Central Asian Muslims and the Muslims of South Asia have all greatly appreciated his poetry and spiritual legacy. His poetry has been translated into numerous languages.

Rumi wrote mostly in his native Persian, but occasionally he also used Turkish, Arabic and Greek. His *Mathnavi*, composed in Konya, is universally considered one of the purest 'literary glories' of the Persian language: a six-volume work of poetry regarded by some Sufis as the Persian-language *Qur'an*. It's thought by many to be one of the greatest examples of mystical poetry, and contains approximately 25,000 verses.

Rumi's works are still widely read in their original language across Greater Iran and the Persian-speaking world, while translations remain in Turkey, Azerbaijan, the United States and South Asia.

On the *Mathnavi*, Idries Shah concurs with the general view that:

Rumi's major work, generally considered to be one of the world's greatest books, is his *Mathnavi-i-Maanavi (Couplets of Inner Meaning* ... [but] ... his table-talk (*Fihi Ma Fihi*), letters (*Maktubat*),

---

[6]See the collection edited by Helminski (2000).

Diwan, and the hagiography *Munaqib El-Arifin*, all contain important parts of his teachings.[7]

The *Mathnavi* was a Sufi masterpiece started during the later years of Rumi's life. He began dictating the first volume around the age of 54, in about the year 1258, and continued composing verses until his death in 1273. The sixth and final book remains incomplete. Each book consists of about 4,000 verses and contains its own prose introduction and prologue. The *Mathnavi* can be divided into three groups of two because each pair is linked by a common theme: books 1 and 2 are principally concerned with the *nafs*, the lower carnal self, its self-deception and evil tendencies; books 3 and 4 share the principal themes of reason and knowledge, personified by Rumi in the biblical and Qur'anic figure of the Prophet Moses; and books 5 and 6 are joined by the universal ideal that man must deny his physical earthly existence to understand Allah's existence.

These ideas spoke to me, especially the idea that the 'self' has to be subordinated and controlled in order to reach Allah, and that we are more than our mere physical existence.

The general theme of Rumi's thought, like that of other mystic or Sufi poets of Persian literature, is essentially that of the concept of *tawhid* – union with his beloved (the primal root) from which/whom he has been cut off and become aloof – and his longing and desire to restore it. Rumi believed passionately in the use of music, poetry and dance as a path for reaching Allah. It was from these ideas that the practice of the 'whirling dervishes' developed into a ritual form.

---

[7]Idries Shah (1974), *The Way of the Sufi*, London: Penguin Books, p.110.

Indeed, his teachings actually became the basis for the Mevlevis, which his son Sultan Walad formed. In the Mevlevi tradition, *samā* represents a mystical journey of spiritual ascent through mind and love to the Perfect One. In this journey, the seeker symbolically turns towards the truth, grows through love, abandons the ego, finds the truth and arrives at the Perfect.[8] The seeker then returns from this spiritual journey, with greater maturity, to love and to be of service to others.

Sufism first came to me in book form in the shape of Rumi; however, I then met Shaykh Mohamed Gah Ali, a living advocate of Sufism. I was attending the local mosque and enjoyed the relaxed and beautiful atmosphere. I saw that many people visited this shaykh, some foreigners and indeed quite a number of Jewish converts. I would later observe them in *hadra*, repeatedly reciting the names of Allah. I knew very little of Sufism and was only beginning to understand the true meaning of Rumi's thinking.

By this time I'd left the houseboat and my Norwegian companion, Trond, behind, and was staying in a nearby small guesthouse. The owner's son began to tell me a little about the shaykh and he suggested I meet him in person at the mosque after *maghrib* (prayers). The mosque was more like a small house – unlike the elaborate structure of the nearby Masjid of Akhund Mullah – and people would come and give money to the shaykh. When I arrived for our prearranged meeting I immediately discovered that he didn't speak any English, so someone translated for me, and I suspect the translation was poor. Shaykh Ali was Indian born, perhaps in his middle to late seventies, and possessed a remarkable white beard which, close up, appeared almost crystal-coloured.

---

[8]Shah (1974), *op. cit.*, p. 112.

The first time I attended a *hadra* at the mosque, all the lights were turned off and all I could see was the name of Allah written in white on the near wall. This collective ritual involved the almost endless recitation of *Allah*, followed by repetitive breathing rhythms. In my *tariqa* (Sufi order), the Shadhili – a Sufi order of Sunni Islam founded by Abul Hasan Ali ash-Shadhili – we stand when reciting, and do not sway or dance, as do some other *tariqas*. So we just stand, don't move around in a circle, but it nonetheless remains joyous. The important aspect is how the follower, the seeker (*murid*), perceives it: if one's heart and soul aren't in it, it won't work; it will mitigate the power of collective energy. We would do such things as speak one thousand recitations and then the Shaykh would give a lesson. Memorably, the first lesson of Shaykh Ali that I heard was that of *Ashabu Al-Kahf*.

Verses 9–26 of the Qur'an tell the story of the 'People of the Cave' (*Ashabu Al-Kahf*). The narrative is as follows: a number of young believers lived at a time when they were persecuted for their beliefs. Upon the guidance of their Lord, they fled this city where believers were prosecuted, and took refuge in a cave where they soon fell asleep. According to the Qur'an, they slept for 309 years, and when they woke they found that the people of the city had become believers. For me, the way he told the story was an absolute revelation, the way he brought the Qur'an to life. I'd heard nothing like it ever before.

The shaykh explained the Qur'an in a completely different way from everything I felt I knew. His manner of teaching was through the telling of 'stories', and he presented beautiful lessons. In contrast, in Kuwait and Jordan all we ever learned from the Qur'an were the many rules we had to follow, the numerous prohibitions to be aware of, the many painful punishments that could be meted out, the descent into Hell, and so on. But the shaykh's Qur'an was beautiful.

One day Shaykh Ali suggested I visit Shaykh Hussein in Sonamarg ('Meadow of Gold'), a hill station in the Ganderbal district of the Indian state of Jammu and Kashmir. Here lie the great Himalayan glaciers of the Kashmir Valley, namely the Kolhoi Glacier and the Machoi Glacier, with peaks of 5,000 metres (16,400 feet), such as Sirbal, Kolhoi, Amarnath and Machoi. Sonamarg, an alpine valley, is a popular tourist destination, nestled within these imposing Himalayan peaks. In the winter months, people would be found in the valley, and then in the summer would travel up to the mountains. Shaykh Hussein spent his time, I was told, with people there, 'healing them'.

Sadly, and with humility, I have to say that I didn't learn too much from him. For the villagers he was like a doctor. But everyone knew or assumed his 'healing' actually came from his father, also a shaykh in Sonamarg. The younger shaykh was merely the conduit, the messenger, not the message.

I travelled to the mountains, along with my small canvas tent, and when I got there I didn't know how to assemble it! I took lots of photos there, including many of Shaykh Hussein. My first impression of him was that he was so young. Then I realised he was less a man of knowledge and more a man of touch, of healing, of transmission from his father. In fact, I did spend a little time with his father and he did teach me a few things about healing and, invariably, about Sufism.

Slowly, but inexorably, I felt I was beginning to understand the mystical way of Islam.

*

I continued my journey and made my way to Kye Gompa, a Tibetan Buddhist monastery located on top of a hill at an altitude of 4,166 metres (13,668 feet) above sea level, close to the Spiti River, in the Spiti Valley of Himachal Pradesh. It's the biggest monastery in Spiti Valley and was a religious training centre for lamas.

Kye Gompa is said to have been founded by Dromtön (Brom-ston, 1008–1064 CE), a pupil of the famous eleventh-century teacher Atisha. In the past, Mongol armies destroyed it, and then in 1841 it suffered more damage from a Sikh army; in 1975 a violent earthquake caused even further damage.

I hadn't made an appointment or contacted the monastery. I simply calculated the distance to get there, worked out the easiest route and just arrived, unannounced. When I went inside and entered the monastery – with very little being said to me – I noticed that the walls were covered with paintings and murals, apparently an example of the fourteenth-century monastic architecture, a result of Chinese influence. There were three floors, the first one mainly underground and used for storage. One room, called the Tangyur, was painted with wonderful murals. And the ground floor was the beautifully decorated Assembly Hall, which also contained numerous cells for the monks.

I stayed at Kye for over a week and experienced considerable tranquillity and a sense of peace. What I humbly began to call my mystic way of life was gathering pace. By this time I'd completely stopped smoking dope and my transition to this other mystical way was slow and peaceful, but seemingly inevitable.

At Kye I slept on a concrete bed. Indeed, even the so-called 'pillow' was made of a type of concrete material. The routine I followed was as follows: we were woken at five in the morning and given some butter tea, which tasted absolutely disgusting. Then we meditated and performed the 'cat' yoga pose. We'd stay in this position for about 40 minutes. The Master would then hit my spine with a very thin stick and, because I was naked from the waist upwards, the blood would flow up into my head, which was a strange but somehow satisfying experience. We would then perform the lotus position. What followed was a meal that was called 'breakfast'.

In my free time, away from this highly structured routine, I would sit quietly in the corner as the monks continued to pray. I also used the Assembly Hall for prayer, and would perform the *adhan*, make my prayers and then be still. The Buddhist monks were interested in what I did, but there wasn't much of a shared language, so we would gracefully and silently smile at one another.

I was in such a state of peace. I was searching internally for answers, for truth and for some sense of certainty, but I remained in peace. I desperately wanted to stay in India and explore more – for example, to discover more about Buddhism and Hinduism. I wanted to read more, think more. My heart belonged to India, especially Kashmir and the mountains. However, I was also thinking about the future, and was contemplating what to do with the rest of my life.

India had calmed me down. Unlike some travellers to India, I'd stopped, not started, smoking dope and other drugs. In terms of the future, one of the things I was certain of was that I wanted to legalise my status. So I decided I'd apply for UK citizenship via the refugee route. But first, I would return to Jordan.

*

On arrival in Jordan, I applied for a job at the prestigious and newly constructed Le Royal Hotel in Amman, which had been built with Iraqi money. The Irish-born Head of Food and Beverages had also studied at Queen Margaret's in Edinburgh, so he was amenable to giving me a job.

I began at Le Royal, and while I was busy working and also attending the mosque, my mum announced that at the age of 32 it was time for me to marry, that she had found me someone who she believed would make a 'good' wife. I was, of course, surprised and shocked, but also respectful of her decision. She wore *hijab* and her name was Iman. I was used to the *hijab*, as my mum and sister wore them, and so later, when I visited Iman, she'd take off the *hijab* in my presence, something that didn't come as a surprise.

Iman came from a 'nice' family, was middle-class and her brothers worked successfully in the USA. I obediently went with my dad to meet her and her family. After some discussion of details, I agreed with the proposed arrangement and said, 'Okay, let's get engaged.' However, her family said no and demanded that first I must agree a date for the marriage – as her mother said, I had to first 'sign the book', the *el-kitab*. So we agreed to marry.

*

While working as restaurant manager at Le Royal, I was also going to the mosque, called the Educational Islamic College, every morning. It doubled as an educational institution, and King Abdullah had attended. I still couldn't read the Qur'an correctly but, fortuitously, at the college I had the good fortune of meeting Shaykh Mamdouh abu Shamat, Syrian-born but resident in Amman.

When I started performing my prayers more sincerely, I ceased all sexual activity. I thought to myself that if I was going to pray properly I had to focus on that alone. I didn't drink alcohol, and I had ceased to use drugs.

So I began to sit with the shaykh and read the Qur'an. After every single sentence he would correct me. I thought to myself, 'I'm pathetic, I'm thirty-two years old and can't read the Qur'an correctly.' Despite this sense of embarrassment, I stayed with the shaykh every morning after *fajr* (morning prayer) for over eight months, and he taught me how to read the Qur'an properly. I also spent a considerable time simply in his company, visiting people and talking with them about their lives, their problems, and their hopes for the future and their religious beliefs. He was a highly respected man, having taught so many people the correct way to read the Qur'an.

I would visit him at his house and we would read, and he would correct and correct and correct me until I got it right. Of course, I wasn't the only one: perhaps 90 per cent or more of people who try cannot read the Qur'an correctly. It's about interpretation: the way one says words and phrases; the meaning of a word when read; when to start; when to stop. In the fullness of time, I began to be able to recite Qur'an in my heart.

What the shaykh taught me was that I was reading the Qur'an just like I would any other book, and that was wrong. He would spend four hours with me reading just one line. He'd explain so many stories – where they came from, where they were going, how they related to my life. There are no full stops in the Qur'an, so I would learn how and where to stop.

I believed the shaykh loved me. He would always put his hand through mine, and even before I ever climbed a mountain, one day he turned and said, 'You will be something. You will make something of your life.'

I have now memorised parts of the Qur'an well, and always recite a number of passages when I'm sitting in a tent on the mountain, or approaching a peak.

*

The scholar Carl Ernst has read and puzzled over the Qur'an ever since he was at graduate school in the USA in 1975.[9] As with the Bible and other religious tomes, some passages of the Qur'an are 'mild', others 'blistering', and later ones appear to cancel out earlier ones. So it's fair then to ask the question, 'Which has precedence?' Ernst experienced an epiphany when he encountered an ancient literary technique known as 'ring composition'.[10] He explains: 'we read books first page to last, but before cover-to-cover reads there were scrolls, and before scrolls there was oral storytelling'. Many older works, Ernst discovered from a scholar of Hindi-language Sufi texts, were not composed in a straight-line manner; instead, the last line would mirror the first line of a passage, the second the second to last, and so on, and the centre of the passage was where the key statement sat. Why would anyone compose a story that way? Ernst addressed the question and argued that in oral storytelling people had to memorise huge amounts of material.

---

[9]See John Yemma, 'Carl W. Ernst: Reading the Quran in a New Way', *Christian Science Monitor*, 28 September 2012.

[10]Carl W. Ernst (2012 edition), *How to Read the Qur'an*, Chapel Hill: The University of North Carolina Press.

They used mnemonic devices, like that of the 'memory palace', in which a storyteller mentally walks through a palace, each room helping him recall part of the story. That could have influenced where the most important spot would be – perhaps in the palace's centre.

In early written literature, scrolls were common. The ends of a scroll roll up. The centre is the sweet spot. So 'ring composition' was natural in the pre-book era. Indeed, parts of *The Iliad* and parts of the Bible (Leviticus, in particular) appear to use this structure. And so, a few years ago, Ernst began looking for ring composition in the Qur'an. For example, consider Sura 60: verses at the beginning and end deal with Abraham's battle with idol worshippers. But at the centre is the remark, 'Perhaps it may be possible for God to create affection between you and your enemies,' which seems to be a call for tolerance and mercy.

*

My life appeared to be heading in the right direction – a more spiritual and contented existence. But there was still the question of Iman. We'd enjoyed a somewhat lavish and over-the-top engagement party at the Amman Sheraton, but in my heart I knew I couldn't get married. It wouldn't have been fair to her. At the time all that was in my heart was learning the true message of the Qur'an.

So, one bright morning, the sky clear blue, I gave my dad the wedding ring and told him the wedding was cancelled and that I was leaving Jordan. I did the right thing: I let Iman take her *mahr*,[11]

---

[11]*Mahr* is a mandatory payment, in the form of money or possessions paid by the groom, or by the groom's father, to the bride at the time of marriage that legally becomes her property. While the *mahr* is often money, it can also be anything agreed upon by the bride, such as jewellery, home goods, furniture, a dwelling or some land.

which was some gold and 3,000 Jordanian dinar. We divorced
through the courts, where I agreed to pay *metakher*, a divorce
payment to Iman's family.

Coincidentally, I was beginning to hate my job. I was receiving less
money than the foreigners at the hotel, despite doing the same work.
I wanted to get my life together, legalise my UK status and get home –
back to Edinburgh.

*

Much later I discovered that Iman had married and had two children,
both of whom were disabled. That saddened and shocked me and,
selfishly, I wondered if we would have had disabled children if *we'd*
married. But apparently she is happy and lives in Dubai.

5

The Dream

Follow your passion, be prepared to work and sacrifice,
and above all don't let anyone limit your dreams.
MOSTAFA SALAMEH

And, when you want something, all the universe conspires in
helping you to achieve it…[and]…It's the possibility of having a
dream come true that makes life interesting.
PAULO COELHO

Lunar House is a depressing-looking 20-storey office block in Croydon, South London, and houses the headquarters of 'UK Visas and Immigration', a specialist division of the UK's Home Office. The building was completed in 1970 and, in common with a neighbouring building, Apollo House, its name was inspired by the moon landing of *Apollo 11* in 1969. The building's name has become synonymous with immigration matters, and Lunar House is perceived by the British public as the front line of Britain's immigration service because the main Public Enquiry Office (PEO) is based here.

Lunar House has been subject to regular and frequent criticism. For example, in the summer of 2004 it was said to possess 'inadequate child protection procedures, and staff were not alert to the need to ensure that agreed safeguards on the detention of children were implemented,' while another report found that 'minimum standards of comfort afforded to British citizens do not apply to migrants waiting for services at Lunar House ... Areas of immediate concern include the quality of facilities for applicants, the quality and fairness of transactions, the quality of IT and record-keeping and the working conditions of staff.'[1] Access to the building still requires airport-style security checks.

And so it was at this very Lunar House that I began the process of acquiring legal status. I made the journey to Croydon, through lengthy backed-up traffic, with an Iraqi man, the uncle of my Luton friend Mazen. On this miserable rainy day, I presented myself at the desk, ready to begin the interview that would decide whether I was able to remain legally in the UK and gain citizenship.

Once in the room, I sat there, my usual self-confidence ebbing away, and I was asked, 'How did you enter the country?' I managed an oblique and elusive answer. My interview felt more like an interrogation. However, after much quibbling, later that day it became apparent that somehow it had worked and I received the papers I needed. Ultimately, in 2008, I received full UK citizenship.

*

In 2003 I was back in Edinburgh, but with very little money. I returned to start all over. I found a room in a small flat, in Gardiner Crescent, with Jan, a healer who wrote books on her particular techniques. I'd met her a few years earlier in a yoga studio.

---

[1] See http://www.researchasylum.org.uk

Forever wanting to educate and train myself, I enrolled at a college in Wester Hill, to learn sign language. I'd previously met a deaf woman and had been frustrated that we couldn't communicate sufficiently, so I spent the next six months learning the signs, gestures and meanings behind the language. At this time I also did the training for a bodyguard certificate. This was a 10-day course and involved such topics as 'how to use the radio', 'how to *sense* a room', 'taking care of celebrities and VIPs' and, most significantly, 'how to safely and successfully deal with violence'. I thought this qualification and training might come in useful if I ever needed to earn quick money. But, thankfully, I didn't.

I was then offered another job at the Sheraton. But first I want to describe further how mysticism and spirituality, particularly Sufism, had come to underpin my beliefs.

*

Many critics of Sufism focus on what they see as the overpowering role of the shaykh. They'd argue that the follower (*murid*) had to always *obey* the shaykh. That wasn't my experience at all. My shaykh would always ask me to listen to my heart, not him. He would also stress the importance of intention. He'd say the intention was more important than the action itself. Perhaps it is more accurate to suggest that the 'Sufi teacher is a conductor, and an instructor – not a god.'[2] Personality worship is forbidden in Sufism. Hence Rumi: 'Look not at my exterior form, but take what is in my hand'.[3]

---

[2]Idries Shah (1974), *The Way of the Sufi*, London: Penguin Books, p. 33.
[3]*Ibid.*

I'd lost my way completely in the UK and it was only whilst in India that I realised that Allah was in my heart. It was an experience, not just a belief. Allah gives me strength. Everything I do I relate it to Allah. We're trapped in a circle and I always say to myself, 'Every day take yourself out of that circle for five minutes.'

*

India had taught me how little I actually knew about the religion I was born into, and also taught me that I knew nothing of significance about the holy Qur'an. But India also opened my eyes more generally to religion and spirituality, and in particular taught me something about Buddhism and Hinduism. These traditions have also affected the way I behave in my life and what I believe.

Even before I arrived at Kye Gompa monastery, Trond, the Norwegian 'addict', had taught me some Buddhism. I remember late one evening, sitting on the houseboat and watching the sun go down over the lake, he told me a tale which, later, I understood to be quite well known:

There were these two Japanese monks, one old, and the other young. They were making their way home to their monastery, and they came across a river where they found a young woman crying. The younger monk glanced towards her but the older one frowned – 'You mustn't talk with women.' However, the younger monk disagreed. The woman told him the river was too strong for her to cross. So the younger monk suggested he carry her across on his shoulders. The older monk was outraged. When they reached the other side, the woman thanked the younger monk. All the way home the older monk was angry, and as they approached the monastery gates the younger monk turned to him and said: 'I left that woman at the bank of the river, why are you still carrying her?'[4]

This corresponded with all the life-lesson and inspirational literature I'd consumed since my early days with Caroline and Stephen. It was simple, but true. And useful.

After my experience at Kye Gompa, and after more conversations with interested parties, and after some further reading – in particular, lots of Alan Watts and Christmas Humphreys[5] – I realised that Buddhism changed an important question for me. Instead of puzzling over the question, 'What is God?' I became equally interested in the question, 'How should we behave?'

Worldwide, there are 376 million followers of Buddhism. Buddhists seek to reach a state of *nirvana*, by following the path of Siddhartha Gautama, who went on a quest for enlightenment around the sixth century BC. Buddhists have no belief in a personal god, and believe that nothing is fixed or permanent and that change is always possible. The path to enlightenment is through the practice and development of morality, meditation and wisdom. Buddhists believe that life is both endless and subject to impermanence, suffering and uncertainty. Existence is endless because individuals are reincarnated over and over again, experiencing suffering throughout many lives. It is impermanent because no state, good or bad, lasts forever. Our mistaken belief that things can last is a major cause of suffering.

---

[4]Oral tradition.

[5]Alan Watts' *The Way of Zen, Nature, Man and Woman, Tao Te Ching*, and Christmas Humphreys' *Buddhism*, and *The Wisdom of Buddhism*.

Siddhartha Gautama, the Buddha, was born into a royal family in present-day Nepal over 2,500 years ago. He lived a life of privilege and luxury until one day he left the royal enclosure and encountered, for the first time, an old man, a sick man and a corpse. Disturbed by this, he became a monk and soon after adopted the harsh poverty of Indian asceticism. Neither path satisfied him and he decided to pursue the 'Middle Way' – a life without luxury but also without poverty. Buddhists believe that one day, seated beneath the Bodhi tree ('the tree of awakening'), Siddhartha became deeply absorbed in meditation and reflected on his experience of life until he became 'enlightened'. By finding the path to enlightenment, he was led from the pain of suffering and rebirth towards nirvana and became known as the Buddha or 'awakened one'.

Ever since leaving Kuwait at 18, and certainly while in the UK and Jordan, I had always felt that it was my responsibility to make a good or bad life. No one else could do it for me. So Buddhism 'spoke to me'. Just consider some of the better-known quotes of Siddhartha:

No one saves us but ourselves. No one can and no one may. We ourselves must walk the path.

Work out your own salvation. Do not depend on others.[6]

*

Any traveller to India encounters Hinduism, in all its bizarre glory. It's the religion of the majority of people in India and Nepal, with around 80 per cent of Indians describing themselves as Hindu. It also exists

---

[6]Oral tradition.

among significant populations outside the subcontinent and has over 900 million adherents worldwide.

I remember walking along a Delhi street and encountering a huge, noisy celebration. A large group of men were carrying an enormous, pink-coloured elephant, which had just one tusk. I asked someone what it meant: he immediately pointed to a tiny mouse-like creature under the elephant's foot. He elaborated, and told me that it was 'the elephant-headed god called Ganesha. We pray to Ganesha before making any important decision.' I asked this wildly enthusiastic man, his face covered in some kind of powder, what the symbolism of the one tusk meant.

> After a feast the greedy Ganesha went for a ride on a rat. A snake frightened the rat and Ganesha fell, his stomach bursting open. He gathered up his stomach and used the snake as a belt to hold himself together. The moon saw this and laughed. So, an angry Ganesha tore off a tusk and threw it at the moon.[7]

I discovered, that same afternoon, that there are as many interpretations of the significance of the one tusk as there are Hindu gods. In other words, many! I also discovered that this particular deity is much favoured by small children, as well as adults.

Hinduism resists easy definition partly because of its vast array of practices and beliefs. It's also closely associated with the other Indian religions of Sikhism, Buddhism and Jainism. I've already mentioned the concept of *equanimity*, but I also discovered other aspects to the Jain way of thinking that greatly appealed to me – most obviously, that of *ahimsa*. This idea – not a command, just a suggestion to adherents – that

---

[7]For an account of this god, see S. Jagannathan & N. Krishna (1992), *Ganesha*, London: Vakils Feffer and Simons.

one should respect all living creatures and desist from acting violently towards them tested my way of thinking, and eating.

Unlike most other religions, Hinduism has no single founder, no single scripture, and no commonly agreed set of teachings. For these reasons, writers often refer to Hinduism as a 'family of religions' or 'way of life'. The term itself, Hindu, was derived from the river or river complex of the northwest, the Sindhu (a Sanskrit word used by the inhabitants of the region, the Aryans, in the second millennium BC). The term 'Hindu' as we know it probably doesn't go back before the fifteenth and sixteenth centuries, when it was used by people to differentiate themselves from followers of other traditions, especially the Muslims (*Yavannas*) in Kashmir and Bengal. At that time the term may have simply indicated groups united by certain cultural practices such as cremation of the dead and styles of cuisine.

We can't define Hinduism according to belief in concepts such as *karma* and *samsara* (reincarnation) because Jains, Sikhs and some Buddhists also accept this. However, we can say that it is rooted in India, that most Hindus revere a body of texts as sacred scripture known as the *Veda*, and that most Hindus draw on a common system of values known as *dharma*. Also, we can add that most Hindus believe in a Supreme God whose qualities and forms are represented by the multitude of deities which emanate from 'him' – Vishnu, Rama, Kali, Yama, Vasu, Indra, Rudras, Ganesha, Sita, Rama, Jai, Hari, Shiva, Devi, the list is endless. Indeed, there are major deities and minor ones, and subsidiary minor ones, and so on. Hindus also believe that existence is a cycle of birth, death and rebirth, governed by *karma*, and that the soul passes through a cycle of successive lives, with each incarnation always dependent on how the previous life was lived.

When I first encountered these ideas, they were alien to me. Islam, the religion of my birth, offers considerable certainty, but Hinduism was totally different. In my experience, however, it was a religion of joy that appeared to govern almost every decision and waking hour of the average Indian.

*

But Sufism had touched my heart.

What is it exactly? It's usually described as 'mystical Islam'. Indeed, Islamic scholar Martin Lings argues that Sufism, or *Tasawwuf*, as it is known in the Muslim world, 'is Islamic mysticism'.[8] However, some people believe that what we've come to know as Sufism had its roots *prior* to Islam,[9] and that it is possible to separate out its ideas and practices. This, however, is a minority view. A number of Rumi's poems, for example, suggest the importance of outward religious observance for Sufis, and the primacy of the Qur'an.

> Flee to God's Qur'an, take refuge in it
>
> there with the spirits of the prophets merge.
>
> The Book conveys the prophets' circumstances
>
> those fish of the pure sea of Majesty.[10]

Sufism has always been associated with peacefulness, the unmediated attempt at a form of closeness with God, and the centrality, the primacy, even, of love. It is also believed that the adherent, the

---

[8]Martin Lings (1999), *What is Sufism?*, London: The Islamic Texts Society, p. 15.
[9]For example, this is the argument of Irina Tweedie. See her (1995) *Daughter of Fire: A Diary of a Spiritual Training with a Sufi Master*, San Francisco: The Golden Sufi Centre.
[10]Shah (1974).

follower, the *murid*, will be greatly tested in their pursuit of self-understanding. Unquestionably Sufism is in a sense 'beyond words'. It is experiential. As my shaykh said to me, 'If you'd never before tasted an onion, how would I be able to describe that taste to you? So, how can I describe love...'

Many Sufi practices centre on the recitation and remembrance of Allah. As stated in the Qur'an, 'hearts become tranquil through the remembrance of Allah'.[11] Indeed, it is believed that chanting the names of Allah like a mantra, as well as performing meditative exercises, will induce an altered state of consciousness and enable the seeker to 'catch a glimpse of God by cultivating a different mode of perception'.[12]

Sufis are aware that one of the names of the Prophet was *Dhikr Allah* (Remembrance of God). *Dhikr* as practised by Sufis is the invocation of Allah's divine names, verses from the Qur'an, or sayings of the Prophet in order to glorify Allah. *Dhikr* is encouraged either individually or in groups and is a source of tranquillity for Sufis.

Being relatively uneducated, introduced to Sufism firstly through the poetry of Rumi, and thereafter by association with a number of shaykhs in India and Jordan, I was both intellectually and emotionally challenged by the snippets of Sufi wisdom I encountered.

Sin against God is one thing; but sinning against man is worse.
Sufian Thauri

Do not regret the past and do not worry about the future.
Dhun-Nun

---

[11] Verse 13:28.
[12] Karen Armstrong (2010), *The Case for God*, London: Vintage Books, p. 135.

Being a Sufi is to put away what is in your head – imagined truth, preconceptions, and conditioning – and to face what may happen to you.

Abu Said

You possess only whatever will not be lost in a shipwreck.

El-Ghazali

Sleep with the remembrance of death, and rise with the thought that you will not live long.

Uwais El-Qarni

Knowledge is better than wealth. You have to look after wealth; knowledge looks after you.

Ali

People tend to want to study under famous teachers. Yet there are always people not considered distinguished by the public who could teach them as effectively.[13]

El-Ghazali

But it didn't take me long to realise that there was a connection, a similarity, between the life-lesson and inspirational literature I'd read and the seemingly psychological dimension to Sufism.

Non-Muslims often mistake Sufism as a 'sect' of Islam, but it's more accurately described as an 'aspect' of Islam. Sufi *tariqas* (orders) can be found among both Sunni and Shia but also other Islamic groups. The Shadhili *tariqa*, to which I belong, has historically been of importance and influence throughout North

---

[13]Shah (1974).

Africa and Egypt. Among the figures most known for their literary and intellectual contributions are Ibn 'Ata Allah, author of the *Hikam*, and Ahmad Zarruq, author of numerous commentaries and works, and in poetry there have been the notable contributions of Muhammad al-Jazuli, author of the *Dala'il al-Khayrat*, and Busiri, author of the famous poem the *Qaṣīda al-Burda*. And it's been suggested that the Shadhili school, through Ibn Abbad al-Rundi, was influential on St John of the Cross, in particular his account of the 'dark night of the soul'.[14]

Sufis are emphatic that Islamic knowledge should be learned from teachers and not exclusively from books. *Tariqas* can trace their teachers back through the generations to the Prophet himself – 'a guarantee of authentic wisdom via an unbroken line of spiritual teachers going back to the Prophet'.[15] Modelling themselves on their teachers, students hope that they too will glean something of the Prophetic character. Additionally, in a similar way to early Christian desert asceticism, the serious seeker lives over a period of time alongside the teacher. Indeed, it is the *interpersonal* process of closeness with the teacher (shaykh) and the *experiential* discipline, rather than intellectual knowledge, that is key to reaching mystical depths.[16]

Although Sufis are relatively few in number they have helped shape Islamic thought and history. Through the centuries, Sufis contributed hugely to Islamic literature, and Rumi, Omar Khayyám and Al-Ghazali's influence extended beyond Muslim lands, to be quoted by

---

[14]Suggested by the Spanish scholar Miguel Asín Palacios (1871–1944).
[15]Philip Sheldrake (2012), *Spirituality*, Oxford: Oxford University Press, p. 47.
[16]*Ibid.*

Western philosophers, writers and theologians. And Sufis were also
influential in spreading Islam, particularly to the furthest outposts of
the Muslim world in Africa, India and the Far East.

Several origins of the word *Sufi* have been suggested. It may derive
from the word for wool and the woollen garments worn by early Sufis.
It may also have connections with the word for purity, and another
suggestion is that it has links with the Greek word *Sophia*, or wisdom.

However, throughout history a Sufi was most often understood to
be a person of religious learning who aspires to be close to Allah.[17]
Sufis could also be described as simply 'devout Muslims', something
easy to assert but less easy to achieve; they would have to call to mind
'the divine presence when they performed such ordinary actions as
eating, washing, preparing for bed, praying, almsgiving and greeting
each other', and in addition they must 'guard their ears from slander
and obscenity; their tongues from lies; they must refrain from cursing
or sneering at others'.[18] If that were not challenging enough, the
'devout (or "good") Muslim' would also ensure that they did not harm
another creature, and make certain that their hearts remained free of
envy, anger, hypocrisy and pride. But, in the end, the Sufi is distinctive
in nurturing theirs and others' spiritual dimension.

Idries Shah observes that Sufis state that 'there is a form of
knowledge which can be attained by man, which is of such an order
that it is to scholastic learning as adulthood is to infancy', and he
recalls the remark of El-Ghazali, who argued that, 'A child has no
real knowledge of the attainments of an adult. An ordinary adult

---

[17]See Shah (1974).
[18]Armstrong (2010), p. 136.

cannot understand the attainment of a learned man. In the same way a learned man cannot understand the experiences of enlightened saints or Sufis.'[19] Shah adds that Sufism can be taught in many guises, in which 'some quite happily use a religious format, others romantic poetry, some deal in jokes, tales and legends, yet others rely on art-forms and the products of artisanship', and concludes that:

> Sufis have been judicially murdered, hounded out of their homes or had their books burned, for using non-religious or locally unacceptable formulations. Some of the greatest Sufi classical authors have been accused of heresy, apostasy…[and]… even political crimes.[20]

*

This courage to formulate a personal belief, a personal formulation of Islam, again spoke to me.

At this point I was back working, again in a managerial role at the Sheraton, and housed in a new flat in Montpelier Place, in the Bruntsfield district of the city. I shared the flat with an Irish girl I worked with at the Sheraton, and we lived together simply as friends.

India had calmed me, focused me and made me feel more at peace with myself. There was no question that India was definitely some kind of turning point.

I continued to read, mainly more life-lesson literature, but also books about people who interested me – inspiring people such as Michelangelo. I was certain that I didn't want to return to Jordan.

---

[19]Shah (1974), p. 28.
[20]*Ibid.*, p. 33.

Then, as now, I truly believed that things happen for a reason, and India had in some sense opened me up to the world, to new possibilities, and had ignited my spiritual and mystical life. And in January 2004 I was fortunate to have another life-changing experience.

*

It was a normal party evening, with a lot of dancing, no drugs, and most of all in the spirit of friendship and joy. This enjoyable evening took place in Glasgow, and afterwards I returned directly to the Sheraton, in Edinburgh, to start work. The following day was the opening of the hotel's newly refurbished in-house restaurant, Santini (now called One Square).

After a hard night partying and a hard day's work – in preparation for the opening – I returned home to Montpelier Place and to Erin, the Irish colleague I was sharing the flat with. I'd invited a number of friends to the opening of Santini, and went to bed, exhausted.

Then, in the middle of the night, I awoke startled, following a particularly vivid, almost Technicolor, dream. I was sweating, having palpitations, and totally perplexed. In this dream it appeared that I was standing on the top of the universe, on top of the world, and I was making the *adhan* (call to prayer). The dream concluded with me on my knees, making my prayers.

After the dream I couldn't get back to sleep. Instead, I paced the flat, still confused, startled, but strangely excited. I sat at the kitchen table, powered up the computer and googled the 'highest place on earth'. Before too long I came across Everest. Despite it being early in the morning I telephoned a friend, Mark Oldham, who I knew had some experience of sports in general and trekking in particular.

After I told him about my dream, he said, 'You're mad – what on earth are you talking about?!' After his initial burst of disbelief, he told me that if I wanted to climb *anything* I should train and begin to read and learn some basics about climbing. I finished the call and then continued to read about Everest.

Somehow this crazy idea that was forming inside my brain – namely climbing the world's highest mountain – suited my personality and worldview. I was always wanting to do something different, was always restless, read numerous inspiring autobiographies and, perhaps more importantly, being an employee never really suited me, even when my working conditions were agreeable. I always felt the urge to 'go it alone'.

I'd never lacked self-confidence or what might be called courage; I was always prepared to take risks. Perhaps having to become the 'oldest boy' in the family after my brother's accident contributed to this, and certainly making my way from Kuwait to Jordan at the age of 18 was another factor.

*

That evening, after finishing my shift at the opening of Santini, I sat with the friends I'd invited. I remember talking about when I used to spar with boxers at the Palestinian Liberation Organization's office in Kuwait, and how I'd also done some sparring in London and Scotland. And I recall being excited when learning about the new Fight Club in Glasgow. A good friend, Benji, a deputy headmaster, said, 'So, with all this boxing you've done, why don't you do the Fight Club?' I immediately said, 'I can't, I'm going to climb Mount Everest – in the name of peaceful Islam.' Benji's response was to ask me whether I was 'under the influence'. I also remember one of my good friends, Brendan Miles, saying that it was like someone saying, 'I'm going to swim the Channel, but I can't swim.' So people just kept laughing at my 'crazy dream'. However, someone also said that they'd heard that dreaming about mountains symbolised a 'higher realm of consciousness, knowledge and spiritual truth'.

As the evening revelries continued, and my friends saw that I remained serious about the idea, some began to make helpful suggestions. But I suspect, in their hearts, they didn't really take me seriously.

I can't explain it, but I knew that climbing Everest was what I had to do. So, I contacted the *Scotsman* and told them about the dream and my decision. They seemed interested and said they'd send someone round to the Sheraton to talk to me.

The journalist was attentive and appeared genuinely interested. The article appeared soon afterwards:

At first sight, on meeting Mostafa Mahmoud Salameh amid the wood-panelling and muzak of Edinburgh's Sheraton Grand hotel, where he is assistant food and beverage manager, there is little in the be-suited figure to suggest he might become the first Arab to climb Mount Everest [from the South Side]. If and when he does eventually raise the Jordanian flag on the 29,029 ft. summit of Everest – and if single-minded determination was the only yardstick, there would be little reason why he shouldn't – he believes he will be the first Arab to climb the world's highest mountain… But that moment of exhilaration on the summit will be just the beginning, he says, of a one-man, two-way awareness-heightening exercise, to broaden the outlook of what he believes to be the too inward-looking view prevalent among Arab countries and also of a West whose image of Arabs is coloured by ignorance and the more tragically headline-grabbing aspects of the Middle East.[21]

The article continued to highlight the disbelief I encountered in Amman and quoted me as saying that, yes, 'everyone back home' was surprised when I said I was going to climb Everest. The interviews on Jordanian TV would say, 'Is that true? You're going to kill yourself? Why are you doing this?' More importantly, the *Scotsman* article focused on the wider context of the proposed climb, quoting me as saying:

> To climb Everest is something I would love to do, but beyond that, my dream is to…open up the minds of the next generation in Jordan and the Middle East to exactly what's going on in the world. We need to see the bigger picture, because everything in the Middle East, all the political things and the fighting, stop people from taking the broader view. They hate the West for what is happening, but they cannot see the whole picture. I want them to see the whole picture and also to see a bit of the adventure in life, not just politics, politics.[22]

The article continued to comment on some of my qualifications, including my language skills in English, Japanese, Arabic and deaf signing, which I find useful as a universal language when travelling,

[21]*Scotsman*, 'Shout it from the Mount', 28 February 2004.
[22]*Ibid.*

and also the aerobics certificate and intermediate qualification as a bodyguard.

The journalist then noted that Everest is a huge challenge and an unforgiving mountain, as the 120 frozen corpses that lie on the mountain testify. He concluded the article by saying that, although I worked out regularly, I had no ice-climbing skills and had never ever 'climbed with oxygen'.

The journalist then thought he'd come up with an interesting creative opportunity when he sent a photographer to capture me climbing Edinburgh's legendary Arthur's Seat.

*

This hill has a passing mention as one of the sights of Edinburgh in Mary Shelley's *Frankenstein*, and the highly successful 2009 novel *One Day* by David Nicholls features the main characters, Emma and Dexter, climbing Arthur's Seat following their university graduation. In Jules Verne's novel *The Underground City* (or *The Child of the Cavern*), Nell, a young girl who lives in Verne's 'Underground City', is taken to Arthur's Seat to view her first sunrise. She's never before been above ground and is being acclimatised to it. Arthur's Seat is also featured in several of Ian Rankin's Rebus novels.

It's the main peak of the group of hills in Scotland which form most of Holyrood Park, described by Robert Louis Stevenson as 'a hill for magnitude, a mountain in virtue of its bold design'.[23] Situated in the city centre, it lies about a mile to the east of Edinburgh Castle and gives excellent panoramic views of the city. It is relatively easy

---

[23]Robert Louis Stevenson (1879), *Edinburgh: Picturesque Notes*, p. 21.

to climb, and is popular for hillwalking. Many claim that its name is derived from the legends about King Arthur, such as the reference in *Y Gododdin*. There is no traditional Scottish Gaelic name for Arthur's Seat, but William Maitland proposed that the name was a corruption of *Àrd-na-Said*, implying the 'Height of Arrows', which over the years became Arthur's Seat (perhaps via 'Archer's Seat').[24]

So there I stood with the *Scotsman*'s photographer on Arthur's Seat, puffing and panting, completely out of breath after the short and non-demanding climb. I was so unfit, indeed far less healthy and agile than the elderly photographer. When he asked if I could climb higher, I laughed in his face. In the end he took the shot by lying on the ground, thus exaggerating and distorting my height on the hill. When my friends eventually saw the photo in print they all said, 'How on earth did you get up there?'

After the short burst of publicity cooled, I then had to face the difficult task of actually raising finance for my proposed trip. It didn't ever occur to me that I wouldn't be able to actually climb the mountain.

I realised that the only way I could receive substantial support was through an endorsement from King Abdullah of Jordan, who had recently called publicly for Arab youth to 'achieve something' in the world. However, in addition to having no idea as to how I'd reach the king, there was the problem of having absolutely no idea how much such a trip would cost. Again I called my friend Mark Oldham, who suggested I contacted a company called Jagged Globe. I had a lengthy conversation with Jagged Globe and discovered the cost of such a group expedition. Mark also helped me prepare a PowerPoint

---

[24]James Grant (2010), *Old and New Edinburgh*, Charleston, S.C.: BiblioBazaar.

presentation for the royal palace, should an opportunity arise for me to pitch for sponsorship.

*

The *Scotsman* article led to a similar article in Jordan's *Jo* magazine, and within a few weeks the Jordanian Royal Palace called me and politely enquired whether I had ever seriously climbed: 'Are you actually a climber, or a mountaineer?' I gave a sufficiently ambiguous answer. Thereafter, the palace's head of public relations, Moen Khoury, suggested we met in Amman. The first questions he asked were, 'Who are you?', 'Who is your father?', and 'Who do you know of any influence?' It was apparent that he was slightly perturbed that I'd quoted the king in an article without having any personal connection with him. Nevertheless, he appeared quite sympathetic, encouraged by the king's challenge to Arab youth to provide inspiration. He asked me further questions and soon realised that my project was unique, because there were no mountain climbers *at all* in Jordan. I had the impression that he thought the king himself was very supportive of my aims.

I explained to Moen Khoury that I would 'brand' the proposed project as 'From the Lowest to the Highest' and carry out the expedition in the name of peace. He smiled an ambiguous smile, thought about what I'd said, and then told me that he thought the palace would support me financially if first of all I climbed a number of smaller mountains in Nepal, Tibet and North America. This would, obviously, be proof of my determination, commitment, motivation and, most importantly, my level of skill and aptitude.

Enthusiastically, yet still in a state of partial disbelief, I returned to Edinburgh, went to my manager at the Sheraton and asked for unpaid leave. He had obviously seen the publicity and immediately agreed to my request, saying, 'Well done, go for it.'

*

I still had no idea whatsoever of what climbing entailed, what the techniques involved were, and what kind of equipment was required. So I went to a sports shop along the Royal Mile and told them what I was going to do. They laughed aloud and told me that I needed better tents than the ones they sold – 'These are okay for T in the Park or Glastonbury, but not Everest!' One of the guys suggested a shop somewhere in Glasgow, and gave me a lengthy and extensive list of equipment I should buy.

I told my dad about my plan and he didn't take me seriously, although he did say that if he were younger, he'd join me. My mum burst into tears, said she was terrified, and didn't want me to go. Even though news of the proposed trip was building, no one in Jordan took me seriously, although people were sympathetic to the connection between the proposed climb and spreading the message of peaceful Islam.

My plan was to take part in two major training climbs in Nepal and Tibet in the spring and then move to the European Alps in July. Then later that year I would try and climb Shishapangma in Tibet, the world's fourteenth-highest peak. Provided I wasn't dead, in the spring of 2005 I'd make my Everest bid with a group organised by Alpine Ascents.

6

Mount Everest

*The greatest joy in climbing is to be in charge of one's own destiny,
to be out in front, making the decisions, balancing risk.*

CHRIS BONINGTON

*People ask me, 'What is the use of climbing Mount Everest?' and
my answer must at once be, 'It is of no use' … We shall not bring
back a single bit of gold or silver, not a gem, nor any coal or iron…
If you cannot understand that there is something in man which
responds to the challenge of this mountain and goes out to meet it,
that the struggle is the struggle of life itself upward and forever upward, then you won't see why we go. What we get from this adventure is just sheer joy. And joy is, after all, the end of life.*

GEORGE MALLORY

*Courage is not the absence of fear, but rather the judgment that
something else is more important than fear.*

AMBROSE REDMOON

A curious fact is that Ambrose Redmoon was actually the pseudonym
of James Neil Hollingworth (1933–96), beatnik, hippie, writer and
former manager of psychedelic folk rock band Quicksilver Messenger
Service, one of San Francisco's more notable bands. Nevertheless, his

remark about courage has always spurred me on when encountering difficulties or uncertainty.

*

I knew that I was really lucky to receive support from the palace. *I was a nobody.* As I said, I had no *wasta.* So, I travelled to Jordan to finalise the palace's sponsorship and to try and find some more. But, as I was to find out, fund-raising in Jordan is an extremely problematic activity.

Like many other Middle Eastern countries, Jordan operates not through political parties, but through informal networks, and the use of influence or personal and business connections to gain favours, such as jobs or access to goods and services, are covered by *wasta.* Jordan's penal code criminalises corruption, including abuse of office, bribery, money-laundering and extortion, but the government doesn't effectively implement the law. Corrupt public officials are rarely punished, and neither are high-ranking civil servants prosecuted. Demands for so-called 'facilitation payments' and bribery may be encountered, but less frequently than in other Middle Eastern countries.

The Constitution of Jordan states that no member of parliament can have any financial or business dealings with the government, and no member of the royal family can be in the government. However, corruption remains a profound problem.

Jordan is a constitutional monarchy based on the constitution of 8 January 1952. The king signs, executes and vetoes all laws. The king may also suspend or dissolve parliament, and shorten or lengthen any session. A veto by the king may be overridden by a two-thirds vote of both houses of parliament *at his discretion.* He appoints and may dismiss all judges by decree, approves amendments to the constitution, declares war, and commands the armed forces. Cabinet decisions, court judgements and the national currency are issued in his name. The cabinet, led by a prime minister, was formerly appointed by the king, but following Jordanian protests in 2011, King Abdullah agreed to an 'elected cabinet'.

Despite all of this, I received considerable help and sponsorship from the king.

*

It was in April 2004 that I was ready for my first climb. Mera Peak, found in the Mahalangur section of the Himalayas, is a climb of 6,476 metres (21,247 feet), and was first climbed by Roberts and Tenzing in 1953. On a clear day, and from the peak, a climber can see five of the six highest mountains on earth, including Everest, with only K2 in Pakistan out of sight. Before leaving for the climb I'd read that it was a good mountain for those interested in a somewhat 'straightforward introduction to mountaineering'. Apparently, it said, the majority of the ascent involves a walk up a glacier and requires basic 'ice axe and crampon skills'.

I was overloaded with equipment and arrived, after a particularly arduous journey, with three enormous bags, bursting with clothing and equipment, all clearly and unambiguously labelled. There were climbing shoes, a padded fully adjustable harness, a chalk bag, a belay device, semi-rigid 12-point crampons, deadmen (metal plates), ice screws, ice stakes, a carbon-fibre ice axe, waterproof jackets, a balaclava, the list was almost endless. I had absolutely no idea how to use any of this equipment, or what it was for. Before buying the equipment I had never seen any of it previously.

Neil Short, from Jagged Globe, met me at Kathmandu, guffawed and said, 'Why on earth have you brought all this stuff?' I said that I didn't understand any of it, and had just bought what some guy in a shop had told me to buy, and that I'd never even slept in a proper tent before. I added, 'I've never climbed a big hill, let alone a mountain. But, I've paid my money to be on the climb and I just want to get on with it. I've a good attitude and I'm not gonna give you a hard time.' Neil continued to be amused at my lack of preparedness, but I was happy just to be there.

There were eight of us in the team. By this time I was reasonably fit, but only in terms of being able to run for a bus, not to scale a Himalayan mountain. Andy Moffat was on my first climb, and one morning he noticed how tired I was and asked, 'Why didn't you sleep last night?' I answered him that I couldn't because 'I saw a snow leopard yesterday.' He laughed and assured me that there were no snow leopards on the mountain, but I wasn't convinced.

The climb proved really difficult, for me. I constantly felt psychologically and physically miserable and I gave up after I reached 5,400 metres (17,716 feet). I felt sick, tired and thought to myself, 'What am I doing? There's no way I can do this.'

*

I was then booked to climb in Tibet the following month, again with Jagged Globe. So I stayed in Kathmandu for a day or so, travelled to Pokhora and Chitwan to meet the other members of a new team, then set off for Tibet.

The climb was in May 2004. Jagged Globe describes the mountain as follows:

Lhakpa Ri is probably the most attainable 7,000 m peak in the world, located in an amazing situation opposite the North Face of Everest.

The approach is via the Tibetan Plateau to the Rongbuk Monastery and Base Camp on the North side of Everest... The climb itself is across easy-angled glacier then snow slopes, which lead to the north ridge and summit. The ground is moderate, so the climb is feasible for those with previous snow and ice-climbing experiences, who have also trekked at altitudes in excess of 5,000 m before.[1]

The Jagged Globe team expected me to have trained for this climb, especially after I failed at Mera Peak, but I hadn't. I hadn't yet understood the seriousness of what I was attempting.

So, with the help of a terrific and patient guide, Adele Pennington, I began to climb Lhakpa Ri and managed to reach about 6,200 metres (20,341 feet), but then experienced 'snow blindness'. Again, I felt incredibly miserable and depressed. Snow blindness[2] is misunderstood: symptoms include increased tears and a feeling of pain, something like having sand in the eyes. It may be prevented by wearing eye protection that blocks most of the ultraviolet radiation, such as welding goggles with the proper filters, a welder's helmet, sunglasses rated for sufficient UV protection, or the right snow goggles. The condition is usually managed by leaving the source of ultraviolet radiation, covering the corneas and administering medicinal pain relief.

The positives that emerged from the climb were that, thanks to Adele, I learned more about the effects of high-altitude climbing, and from an

---

[1] Promotional material, Jagged Globe.

[2] Photokeratitis, or ultraviolet keratitis, is a painful eye condition caused by exposure of insufficiently protected eyes to the ultraviolet (UV) rays from either natural (e.g. intense sunlight at high altitudes) or artificial (e.g. the electric arc during welding) sources. Photokeratitis is akin to sunburn of the cornea and conjunctiva, and is not usually noticed until several hours after exposure.

older climber, Jack, I gained useful knowledge about my equipment. In fact, his kindness extended to lending me some of his own.

With my proverbial tail between my legs, I returned to Jordan. My financial support from the king extended to my next climb in North America, so I was still on track, if a little disheartened. At the back of my mind was an additional anxiety: with all this travelling, would I have the correct papers so that, when the time came, I could safely return home to Edinburgh? I needn't have worried, as the Royal Palace in Amman ensured that my passport had the correct visas for travel in and out of America.

*

Mount McKinley, as it was called in 2004, is the highest mountain peak in North America, at 6,168 metres (20,237 feet above sea level). Measured by 'topographic prominence', it's the third most prominent peak after Mount Everest and Aconcagua. Located in the Alaska Range in the interior of the US state of Alaska, McKinley is the centrepiece of the Denali National Park. I was soon intrigued by the history of the mountain and its connection with North American native people.

Interestingly, in late August 2015, President Barack Obama officially renamed McKinley, giving it its native name, Denali.[3]

The Koyukon Athabaskan people who inhabit the area around McKinley have always referred to the peak as *Dinale* or *Denali* ('the high one' or 'the great one'). During Russian ownership of Alaska,

---

[3]And immediately, Republican presidential candidate Donald Trump vowed to overturn the decision: 'President Obama wants to change the name of Mt. McKinley to Denali after more than 100 years. Great insult to Ohio. I will change back!' he tweeted.

the common name for the mountain was *Bolshaya Gora* (*bolshaya* = Russian for 'big'; *gora* = Russian for 'mountain'), which is the Russian translation of *Denali*. It was also briefly called Densmore's Mountain in the late 1880s, after Frank Densmore, an Alaskan prospector who was the first European to reach the base of the mountain. And indigenous names for the mountain can be found in seven different Alaskan languages.

In 1896, a gold prospector named it McKinley as political support for then presidential candidate William McKinley, who became president the following year. The United States formally recognised the name Mount McKinley after President Wilson signed the Mount McKinley National Park Act of 26 February 1917. The Alaska Board of Geographic Names changed the name of the mountain to Denali, which is how it was always referred to locally.

*

I flew to JFK, New York, where officials confiscated my ice picks, wallet and other assorted items, as if I planned to use the ice picks as weapons. Perhaps it was because I was an Arab, with Bin Laden still in their minds? After lengthy discussions that entailed me showing these officials paperwork connected to the climb, my items were returned. After this unscheduled delay, I was allowed to travel onwards to Anchorage. When I got to the airport in Alaska, I thought, 'This is the turning point.' I looked around and said to myself, 'Amazing.' My task now was to successfully climb Denali and then receive funding for Everest. I teamed up again with the Jagged Globe people and stayed with other climbers, in a guesthouse owned by a friendly Dutch woman who appeared to be on good terms with all the climbers.

This was the first time I'd been to the USA and everything seemed so big. Sandwiches, plates, cake and, most of all, people. I thought to myself, 'What on earth is going on here!?'

The people I met in Anchorage were friendly and agreeable, if a tad ignorant and naive. For example, I soon discovered that no one knew where Jordan was on the world map, or indeed Israel, and certainly not Palestine. Only Iraq.

After Anchorage I travelled to Talkeetna, the base for any expedition to Denali. This small town of fewer than a thousand inhabitants was also well known for its salmon fishing.

*

In 1906, Frederick Cook claimed the first ascent, which was later proven to be false, and so the first verifiable ascent was achieved on 7 June 1913 by climbers Hudson Stuck, Harry Karstens, Walter Harper and Robert Tatum. The first of them to reach the summit was Walter Harper, an Alaska native. Robert Tatum also made the summit and later commented that the 'view from the top of Mount McKinley is like looking out the windows of Heaven!'[4]

The mountain is now regularly climbed – the climb typically taking two to four weeks and the ascent from base to peak longer than that of Everest – although it's not without its dangers, and indeed by 2003 it had claimed the lives of nearly one hundred experienced mountaineers.

Andy Hall's 2014 book, *Denali's Howl*, tells of the attempt by 12 men to climb the mountain in the summer of 1967, which resulted in the death of 7 of them. On summit day an Arctic 'super blizzard'

---

[4]Colby Coombs and Bradford Washburn (1997), *Denali's West Buttress: A Climber's Guide to Mount McKinley's Classic Route*, Seattle: The Mountaineers Books, p. 26.

closed in, with 'howling 300-mile-an-hour gales'. Hall describes the moment when some of the dead climbers were ultimately found. He describes the body of one of the victims, Mark McLaughlin, whose 'face and hands are blue, green, white, frozen yet decomposing'.[5] He was frozen, wore orange clothes and his face was covered with snow. One of the rescue team, Gayle Nienhueser, remembers finding the body: 'I'd never seen a body before. The hand that was exposed was black, and it had frozen and thawed a couple of times.'[6] Hall makes the point that for the climbers the sight of the corpse was frightening, bringing home the realisation that on Denali, death is never far away for the careless and the unlucky. However, somewhat ironically, it didn't mean that McLaughlin had died a painful death, as 'freezing' can be a relatively painless and peaceful way to die:

> If there is any real pain it comes at the beginning…[and]…fingers, toes, the tip of the nose, earlobes, and other extremities are sacrificed in order to keep the vital organs warm. As the blood retreats to protect the core, feet and hands begin to ache, and the nose and ears sting. Hypothermia takes over when the body temperature slips below 95 degrees Fahrenheit… Hands and feet are soon useless, nose and ears turn white, and lips turn blue, making clear speech impossible.[7]

Hall continues by reporting that when the core temperature reaches 85 degrees Fahrenheit, 'a sudden and inexplicable feeling of heat cascades across the body, so hot that victims often tear their clothes

---

[5] Andy Hall (2014), *Denali's Howl*, London: Bantam Press, p. 155.
[6] *Ibid.*
[7] *Ibid.*, p. 156.

off seeking relief, unintentionally hastening their end'.[8] One theory behind this suggests that the surface capillaries that constricted early on to push body heat into the core suddenly dilate, bringing a burning sensation as blood surges into the newly frozen flesh. Whether it's the body's last-ditch attempt to warm itself or a sudden failure of the muscles constricting the blood vessels is unknown. Hall concludes his gripping account of the disaster by adding that, 'unconsciousness and death usually follow close behind'.[9]

*

Denali was a difficult but, ultimately, successful climb. *And I enjoyed it*. Midway through the climb I did have doubts and thought to myself, 'I'll just go back and work at the Sheraton and never again mention climbing.'

There were two factors that helped me succeed on Denali: one was that I'd acclimatised in Tibet and was continuing to improve as a climber, despite the fact that there were so many things I still didn't understand – like the 'layer system' of clothing. The other factor was that I knew in my heart that 'this was it'. I knew that if I succeeded the king would support my Everest expedition, and if I failed it would be the end of the dream.

Mountaineering is all about the management of self. Managing the body, the heat, the cold, and wearing the right stuff. This is why the layer system is so crucial: air is a good insulator and layered clothing allows air pockets to form where warm air can be trapped. For the same reason, it's important to have windproof clothing that prevents the warm air being blown away.

---

[8] *Ibid.*
[9] *Ibid.*, p. 157.

So after Denali I bought the best-quality clothes, although I still didn't know everything there was to know about layering and other aspects of climbing. For example, previously, like my first climb in Nepal, I'd bought my boots the day before and never broken them in! Someone at Jagged Globe reminded me that when climbing over 5,000 metres (16,400 feet), a climber must know all the equipment. The more I learned about climbing and the equipment and techniques, the more I began to enjoy it.

So, Denali was another life-changing event.

*

When I got back on terra firma, I immediately called Moen Khoury at the royal palace. He said that he was pleased that I'd succeeded in Alaska, and that the king would also be pleased. The news of my success soon appeared in the Jordanian media, with headlines like, 'Jordanian climbs the highest mountain in America.'

King Abdullah II bin al-Hussein, born 30 January 1962, ascended to the throne on 7 February 1999 on the death of his father, King Hussein. He's a member of the Hashemite family, which has ruled the country since 1946 and is descended from the Prophet Muhammad.

Abdullah was born to Hussein and his second wife, the British-born Princess Muna al-Hussein (born Antoinette Avril Gardiner), and was the king's eldest son and, as such, heir apparent to the throne. However, due to the instability of the 1960s, King Hussein decided to appoint his brother, Prince Hassan bin Talal, as his heir, only for the throne to return to Abdullah in 1999. King Abdullah is married to Queen Rania, who is of Palestinian origin and was born in Kuwait.

He began his schooling at the Islamic Educational College in Amman, and then attended St Edmund's School, Hindhead, in England, before continuing his education in the United States at Eaglebrook School and Deerfield Academy in Massachusetts. In 1980 he attended the Royal Military Academy at Sandhurst, was commissioned into the British Army as a Second Lieutenant, and served for a year as a troop commander in the 13th/18th Royal Hussars. He joined the Royal Jordanian Army, and also served with the Royal Jordanian Air Force, where he was trained to fly Cobra attack helicopters.

A few hours after the announcement of his father's death, Abdullah, wearing a red-and-white keffiyeh, went before an emergency session of the Jordanian National Assembly. In Arabic he recited the oath taken by his father almost fifty years earlier, 'I swear by Almighty Allah to uphold the Constitution and to be faithful to the nation.'

The king travels to America and Europe and lectures widely on aspects of democracy and freedom, yet there are some people who believe he should spend more time advancing democracy in his own nation. However, it should be said that the king does much to spread positive messages about Islam to the wider world, for example in the European Parliament.

*

Steve Bell, one of the founders of Jagged Globe, recalls that in 1988 he surmised that if they could take people trekking, what else would it take to go beyond base camp and up the mountains themselves?

So when Jagged Globe eventually announced their 1993 Everest expedition, there was widespread media coverage. They'd assembled a strong team of 11 climbers, and 7 of them, plus 2 guides and 7 Sherpas, reached the summit. As a result, they became the trailblazers for professionally led expeditions, which are the most common form of Everest ascent.

My Everest climb would also be with a professional climbing company, Alpine Ascents, and I was indeed sponsored by the king and also by Jordanian courier company Aramex, whose founder, Fadi Ghandour, put a lot of his own money into my project and efforts.

I was resting in Amman when I realised that this time I really had to undertake some kind of training. My time of acting like an amateur was well and truly over, so I went to Switzerland to learn more about climbing techniques. Kenton Cool, an English mountaineer, alpinist and mountain guide, taught me. One of Britain's leading alpine climbers, he has successfully climbed Mount Everest 11 times, including the occasions when he led Sir Ranulph Fiennes' 2008 and 2009 expeditions.

So I learned how to climb. For example, I learned when and how to use ice picks properly. When I first started climbing, it was all so new to me, completely novel, so difficult, although I always remained positive. I was always the guy in the team taking photographs, laughing and joking, and not taking any of it particularly seriously. Even in Nepal, all the other people in the team were serious. I just took it all day after day, not thinking about crevasses or any other source of danger. I was just happy to be there. But with Everest looming, I changed my mindset and mentality.

And so I climbed Mont Blanc ('White Mountain'), the highest mountain in the Alps and the highest peak in Europe outside of the Caucasus range. It rises 4,810 m above sea level and is ranked eleventh in the world. The first *recorded* ascent was on 8 August 1786, by Jacques Balmat and the doctor Michel Paccard. This climb, initiated by Horace-Bénédict de Saussure, who offered a reward for the successful ascent, usually marks the start of modern mountaineering.

Now, an average of 20,000 mountaineer-tourists ascend the summit each year. It could be considered an easy, yet long, ascent for someone who is well trained and used to the altitude. Nevertheless, each year climbing deaths occur. For example, on 13 August 2014, the bodies of five climbers and their guide were found near Aiguille d'Argentière, a 3,900-metre (12,800-foot) peak, and on the busiest weekends, normally around August, the local rescue service performs an average of 12 missions. Some routes require knowledge of high-altitude mountaineering, a guide and proper equipment. It's a long course that includes delicate passages and the hazard of potential rockslides. Also, at least one night at the refuge is required to acclimatise to the altitude, as less could lead to altitude sickness and possible death.

My time on Mont Blanc was somewhat uneventful. It was a successful ascent, and I continued to learn my craft, but there was nothing unusual in the climb.

*

Then, in the autumn, I travelled to Tibet and, alongside David Hamilton, attempted to climb Shishapangma, also called Gosainthān, the fourteenth-highest mountain in the world. At 8,027 metres (26,335 feet) above sea level, it was the last 8,000-metre peak to be climbed, due entirely to its location within Tibet and the restrictions on visits by foreign travellers imposed by the government of China and the Tibet Autonomous Region. The Sanskrit name of the mountain, Gosainthān, means 'place of the saint' or 'Abode of God'.[10] Up until 2014, 27 people have died climbing the mountain, including Americans Alex Lowe and Dave Bridges, and veteran Portuguese climber Bruno Carvalho. Nevertheless, Shishapangma is one of the easier 'eight-thousanders' to climb.[11]

I didn't actually make it to the peak. I was just too tired, almost exhausted, and suffered considerably from the high altitude. It was, of course, the first time I'd been higher than 7,000 metres (just under 23,000 feet).

*

Tired, but quite relaxed about my failure, I returned to Jordan and, after a short break, set off for Antarctica. The next phase of my pre-Everest training was to try and climb Mount Vinson, the highest peak of the Vinson Massif (group of mountains).

Vinson Massif is a large massif, 21 kilometres (13 miles) long and 13 kilometres (8.1 miles) wide, and lies within the Sentinel Range of the Ellsworth Mountains. It overlooks the Ronne Ice Shelf near the base of the Antarctic Peninsula and is located about 1,200 kilometres (745 miles) from the South Pole. It was discovered in January 1958 by US Navy aircraft. In 2006, it was declared that Mount Vinson and Vinson Massif were separate entities.

Mount Vinson is the highest peak in Antarctica, at 4,892 metres (16,050 feet). It lies in the northern part of Vinson Massif's summit plateau and was first climbed in 1966. It was named after Carl Vinson,

---

[10]Louis Baume (1979), *Sivalaya: explorations of the 8000-metre peaks of the Himalaya*, Seattle: The Mountaineers. pp. 131–32.
[11]www.wikipedia.org

a United States Georgia Congressman, who was a key supporter of funding for Antarctic research.

I flew into Antarctica with the rest of the group, aboard a giant and noisy Hercules plane, traditionally seen transporting troops and military vehicles. We'd been waiting for four days in a poky hotel in Punta Arenas, the capital city of Chile's most southern region, waiting for permission to fly. We were constantly told, 'No, the weather's too bad. No, you're not going today', and so on.

Once aboard the Hercules, we encountered three huge and somewhat indifferent Russian guys. There was also a helicopter in the middle of the plane and one of these Russians was trying to mend some electrical fault by trying to connect two bare wires. It looked amateurish and scary. Another of these Russian guys threw a small bag of food at each of us – a boiled egg, some sweets, that kind of thing – and said, 'Here's your lunch.' I thought to myself, 'I'm paying $12,000 for a return ticket...'

Once on Mount Vinson everything went to plan. It was an amazing experience and a great climb, despite the fact that the team had an inexperienced guide who lost the way at times and created all sorts of problems for us. It *was* cold, with a biting wind, but I embraced it as an essential learning experience.

*

From the very first time I climbed, in Nepal, I always read the Qur'an while on the journey and always prayed. I enjoyed the silence, the tranquillity and the peacefulness. I remember that many prophets came to the mountain for Allah. I also loved meeting the variety of people I encountered on the mountain, all sorts of different people – experienced climbers, novices, the religious and the irreligious, the serious, the humorous, the happy, the sad, the incredibly wealthy, the less wealthy. I could sit with them all, and on the mountain there was no division. The fact that I was travelling the world, to new and distant places, was an added and enjoyable bonus.

Despite the obvious danger involved in all the climbs, I never ever thought about death or feared it. I believed then, as now, *100 per cent*, that my beliefs would prevent me from ruminating over my possible death on a mountain: namely, *the day I die is already written for me, and no one can either delay that particular day or fast-forward it*. I could die on the mountain or on a plane or on a street or in a hospital or somewhere else altogether. So I never worry about death. There are reasons for everything.

*

With the professional tour company, Alpine Ascents, in March 2005, I made my first attempt at climbing Everest. Right from the beginning, I learned a lot about technique and attitude from one of their guides, Vern Tejas, a well-known Alaskan climber. I felt I was now better prepared; I continued to learn, I understood the equipment better and I was acclimatised. It's fair to say that on every climb there are people in the group who are subjectively unlikeable, or you find irritating, and on this trip it was a large and moody guy, whose name escapes me.

Once on the mountain I was doing fine, climbing carefully and steadily, and then I started to experience severe pain in my right knee. I immediately took a handful of anti-inflammatories and this, I later discovered, led to something akin to a stomach ulcer. We called the doctor at base camp, who told me to check my excrement. A short time later I told him it was coloured black and he immediately ordered me down. A Sherpa helped me down to base camp as I was bleeding heavily, and was weak. I only managed to climb to 6,700 metres (21,980 feet).

I returned to Jordan and, despite what I saw as my failure, a huge welcome from both my family and the media. My family, especially my mum, was happy that I was safe. I subsequently stayed in Amman for two months, rested and recovered, then decided to try and continue my rehabilitation by climbing Kilimanjaro, the dormant volcanic mountain in Tanzania. It's the highest mountain in Africa, and rises approximately 4,877 metres (16,001 feet) from its base to 5,895 metres (19,341 feet) above sea level.

I felt that I had to prove to myself that I could actually climb. It was a relatively easy climb, more of a walk, with very few fearful or traumatic moments.

*

Back in Amman, I was a little lost. There was the climbing, of course, but I had allowed my pursuit of spiritual truth to slip. I met an American woman, Shannon, a bubbly girl who loved theatre and was pro-Palestinian. She was working as a journalist, and was also involved in organising a huge project which brought writers and artists to an event at the Dead Sea. I first met her at Books@Café, a café on 'Umar Ibn Al Khattab Street, where many people whiled away the time smoking shisha on the rooftop patio, overlooking the city. The café's music would fight with the calls to prayer that emanated from the numerous nearby mosques.

After a very short time, and on her suggestion, we moved into a flat together. But I told her, 'This is not the USA. We have to get married

RIGHT: Me (far right) aged three with my father and brother Rafat, aged four at the time.

ABOVE: At a school party, 1986.

RIGHT: Graduation day from Queen Margaret University, Edinburgh in 2000 with, from left, Stephen, Andrea, Toni and Mark.

ABOVE: Working for the Jordanian ambassador in London, Belgravia Place, 1993.

ABOVE: My mother and father in Kuwait, 1988.

LEFT: With gurus in Nepal, 2013.

RIGHT: With Mazen Al Saher in Luton, 1995.

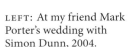

LEFT: At my friend Mark Porter's wedding with Simon Dunn, 2004.

RIGHT: With Mark Manley, Everest Base Camp, 2007.

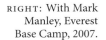

LEFT: At Marcello's Restaurant in Hitchin, 1997.

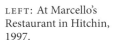

RIGHT: Stephen Torsi, his mother Denise and father Toni. Christmas, 1996.

RIGHT: At the top of Denali, the highest point in North America, 12th June 2004.

BELOW: At Namche Bazaar, Nepal, May 2008 with Rebecca 'the best dentist in the world' fixing my teeth.

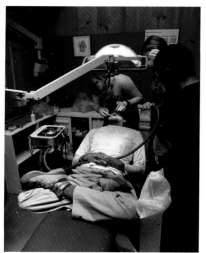

ABOVE: JO magazine cover, February 2004.

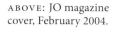

LEFT: With Dr Mike Stroud, Cho Oyu mountain, Tibet, 2007.

LEFT: Climbing an ice fall on Mount Everest, 2008.

BELOW: The Hillary Step, the final stage of the climb before reaching the summit.

ABOVE: The summit of Everest with the Jordanian flag, 25th May 2008, 6:50 a.m.

RIGHT: With Lakpa Tshering, my Sherpa guide, at the highest point in the world.

LEFT: The highest point in South America: Aconcagua, Argentina, February 2008. With my friend Sylvan.

RIGHT: The image of King Hussein of Jordan that I take with me on every expedition. Here on Lobuche East, Nepal in 2014.

ABOVE: In Papua New Guinea en route to climb the highest mountain in Oceania, Puncak Jaya (also known as Cartensz Pyramid), 2012.

RIGHT: Jordanian and Palestinian flags at the North Pole, 2014.

LEFT: At the top of Puncak Jaya, the final mountain of the Seven Summits, November 2012.

BELOW: Receiving a knighthood from His Majesty King Abdullah II of Jordan in October 2008.

LEFT: Sledging towards the North Pole, 2014.

ABOVE: With the BDS (Boycott, Divestment and Sanctions) flag at the North Pole, 2014.

LEFT: With cultural philanthropist Duke Mamdouh Bisharat, 2014.

With Maher Kaddoura in Nepal, trekking to Everest Base Camp for King Hussein's cancer charities.

At the King Hussein Cancer Center, Amman with one of the young patients. Over two million dollars have been raised for the KHCC through our expeditions.

With barrister and activist Mary Nazzal-Batayneh receiving the BDS flag before my trip to the North Pole, April 2014.

LEFT: At a talk for university students as an 'Adventure Ambassador' with Umniah, my sponsor.

ABOVE: With the flag of the King Hussein Cancer Foundation at Everest Base Camp, 2013.

LEFT: Poster for the 'See No Limits' expedition with Suhail Al Nashash (left) and Jarrah Hawamdeh (right).

RIGHT: With my wife Krissy at a friend's wedding, Dublin 2009.

BELOW: With Krissy and our sons Ayman, Yacob and Sami Everest just before leaving for the South Pole, November 2015.

ABOVE: With my son Zaidan in Austin, Texas after completing the Austin Marathon, 2007.

LEFT: With our son Ayman.

RIGHT: At the Landmark Hotel Amman interviewing Dr Mads Gilbert, 2015.

LEFT: At the Mosaic leadership summit, Amman, 2015.

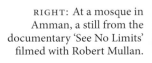

RIGHT: At a mosque in Amman, a still from the documentary 'See No Limits' filmed with Robert Mullan.

if we want to move in together.' So, with very little thought about the consequences, we went to court and got married, then went to the Dead Sea for a three-day 'honeymoon'. My family knew about us, and everything was good.

On our return from the Dead Sea we planned a holiday in India, where I would also continue my training for a second attempt at Everest. Being in India was absolutely wonderful and brought back some good memories.

At this time I also managed to find time to climb Mount Elbrus, in Southern Russia, arguably the highest peak of 'Europe' – a debate I will discuss later.

Back in Amman, Shannon informed me, nervously, that she'd been offered a job back in the USA and wanted to return. I told her that, after my brief experience of the country, I didn't like it and didn't want to go. Then she told me she was pregnant, and, 'Before you ask, I don't want an abortion.' So I went to the USA. To be precise, we lived in Austin, Texas, for about two years, where our son, Zaidan Salameh, was born in January 2007. I didn't like Texas and I didn't like what I came to see as Shannon's 'Americanness' – all drama and control.

Before we'd left for Texas, I'd met Prince Ali (bin Hussein), who was incredibly supportive and provided generous sponsorship, which enabled me to train for a further year in preparation for the next attempt at Everest. So in Austin I went to the gym, did endless and repetitive weights, cardiovascular work, and did some climbing. Increasingly restless, I decided to go to Argentina to climb the highest point in South America, Aconcagua, in the Andes, which peaked at 6,962 metres (22,841 feet). The climb was a personal success. There were 12 of us in the team, yet only two of us actually reached the peak – me and a French climber, Sylvan, who worked for the United Nations in Jordan.

I was extremely happy to have succeeded on Aconcagua, the highest mountain outside of Asia. Like most climbs, the experience was somewhat predictable: standing amid the clouds, taking a few photographs, making a few satellite phone calls, and thinking, 'Now I have to go down.'

Then, when I was ready, I returned to Jordan and attended a gala dinner, hosted by the prince, who gave me the royal flag for my next attempt and also some further sponsorship which, he said, was from his sister, Princess Haya (bint Hussein). His generosity and support I could never forget.

*

My second attempt at Everest took place in 2007. I felt in prime condition and was quietly confident. However, within a short period of time I suffered flu, which subsequently and rapidly developed into a serious chest infection. And after a fall, I also suffered broken ribs. The company I was climbing with was Mountain Madness, which, at the time, seemed somewhat appropriate. I climbed with a Patagonian guide who urged me not to give up the attempt. Despite my poor physical condition and the increasing weakness, I tried and tried. I went down to base camp and came back up, then went down again, then again came up. But my health continued to deteriorate. With a heavy heart I reluctantly abandoned the attempt.

I returned to Jordan. My money was disappearing fast, and I couldn't ask Prince Ali or his sister for more, so I began to sell my own possessions in order to raise some much-needed cash. I needed to support my son, Zaidan, and his mother, Shannon. I sold my car. I had a small mortgage on a house in Luton, and disposed of it and gave it to my friend Mazen. I also had some money in a bank account that I cashed, and I sold a small piece of land in Jordan that I'd bought.

Despite all of this, I never ever thought, 'I can't do this, I'm going to fail.' I just thought that it simply wasn't going to happen that year. As always, I believed that what had happened was for a reason. I also had no difficulty, despite my failure, in facing my sponsors. I said to them, 'I trained well, I tried my best, I had health problems and so had to come down, but I'll try again.' I never tried to explain away the failure. I had actually telephoned Prince Ali from the mountain, said I was sorry and apologised, and he, serenely, simply said, 'Don't worry, we can try again.' His unconditional support was another turning point in my life.

*

As I prepared to undertake my third attempt at Everest, I read Robert Macfarlane's magnificent *Mountains of the Mind* and, in particular, his account of George Mallory's obsession with Everest and *his* three attempts. Macfarlane recounts Mallory's letter to his wife, Ruth, in 1921, in which he admits that the mountain possessed him and had a power over him, and in another letter Mallory asked the question, 'At what point am I going to stop?'[12]

Three times Mallory tried to climb the mountain, in 1921, 1922 and 1924, and the third time he didn't return. Macfarlane concludes his account of George Mallory by fast-forwarding to May 1999, 75 years

---

[12]Robert Macfarlane (2003), *Mountains of the Mind*, London: Granta Books, p. 225.

after he'd disappeared, when a search party discovered his body at an altitude of over 8,000 metres, 'face down on the steep shelves of talus on Everest's north face, his arms flung up and out as though he had halted himself as he slid by digging his nails into the rock'.[13]

> Mallory's clothes had been torn from his corpse by decades of wind and frost, and lay in rags. But the extreme cold had preserved his body. His back still undulated with muscle beneath skin that was bleached bright white. Up there, his body had not putrefied, it had petrified – his flesh looked like nothing so much as stone.[14]

But I didn't fear death, so in March 2008 I again travelled to Everest. My good friend Mark Manley helped me to reach base camp, then he left. I couldn't afford to climb with a large company, so I decided to organise the small team for the climb myself. I took along a Sherpa, Lakpa Tshering, an amazing man from the Khumbu Valley. I'd first met him in 2007, when I was trying to climb Everest for the second time. So, in 2008, I told the people at High Altitude Dreams that I couldn't afford another huge team effort and I wanted to go smaller, but with Lakpa Tshering Sherpa and Changba Nurbu Sherpa.

Lakpa was always fun, full of energy and a family man. It's not plain sailing for Sherpas, as they still have to acclimatise like I did, but their lungpower is stronger because they normally live at something like 4,000 metres (13,123 feet). He would carry more than I did up the mountain, but like any other Sherpa he wasn't necessarily invincible – there are still plenty of dead Sherpa bodies to be seen on the mountain.

---

[13]*Ibid.*, p. 272.
[14]*Ibid.*

In her 1953 book *Coronation Everest*, Jan Morris succinctly describes the qualities of a Sherpa, which I found to be true many years later:

> The Sherpas led a hard, exacting life…[yet]…at any time of day or night your Sherpa would bestir himself to cook your meal, heat your water, carry your pack, climb your mountain. He asked no more than a reasonable fee, and perhaps any old pieces of equipment you had finished with; in return he would do far more than his duties required, giving you always splendid service and good company, and caring tenderly for your health.[15]

On the mountain Lakpa and I talked about Buddhism, Islam, spirituality and religion, family life and children, Jordan, Palestine, Tibet and the Dalai Lama. We never really talked about climbing, although he did tell me about a possible future project of his where he would paraglide from one mountain to another.

Lakpa and I joined a small Nepalese company and shared facilities such as kitchens, and soon afterwards other teams of climbers, from France and Canada, joined in with us. Together we were a contented and congenial group of climbers. One of them was Alan Arnett, who has regularly climbed for causes, mainly for research into Alzheimer's disease.

I'd already made the decision to take the Tibetan flag with me in case I successfully peaked, but had packed it away in a corner in one of my various bags, out of sight. At that time, the Nepalese Army was on the lookout for anyone trying to publicise the Tibetan cause, one I'd become increasingly interested in since my time at the Kye Gompa monastery. In fact, the Nepalese Army had confiscated a flag from

[15]Jan Morris (1958), *Coronation Everest*, London: Faber & Faber, pp. 93–94.

one Canadian and also a 'Free Tibet' T-shirt from another. They had
been escorted off the mountain.

*

Tibet was first invaded and subsequently occupied by communist
China in 1949 – in fact brutally occupied, and its people and culture
ruthlessly exploited and oppressed. Chinese rule in Tibet was only
established after some 400,000 Tibetans died in the so-called 'Twenty
Years War' from 1954 to 1974.

Tibetans are a distinct people, with their own language, culture,
currency, postal system, government and treaties with neighbouring
countries. That freedom, which Tibetans had enjoyed for over two
millennia, was then shattered by China's invasion. For over 60 years
since the illegal military annexation, there has been resistance inside
Tibet to this illegal occupation, waged by Tibetans determined to
regain their independence.

Tibet is three times bigger than Texas, with a population of around
six million, and is situated at the heart of the Asian continent. It has
an average altitude of 4,000 metres (13,123 feet) above sea level, and
forms the major part of the earth's highest mountain range – the
Himalayan-Hindu Kush region.

In the years following China's invasion, many Tibetans fled, forming
an exiled community of over 100,000 Tibetans, based in the USA, Europe,
Canada and Australia, but with the majority living in India. For many
centuries Tibet was headed by the office of the Dalai Lama, through a
series of reincarnations and selection according to Tibetan Buddhist
tradition. However, in 2011 the present Dalai Lama gave up his political
leadership, which is now conferred on an elected prime minister.

About one in five Tibetans has perished under Chinese rule, a similar percentage to the Polish dead of World War II. As the occupation of Tibet violates the terms of the UN Charter, which recognises the right of peoples to determine their own destinies, Tibetans ask why this right should be extended to the Namibian people, the Baltic States and East Timor, but not to them.

*

At 6,700 metres (22,000) feet the Nepalese Army were searching everyone, for flags. By the time I was at that height I'd carefully hidden my flag inside a packet of medical wet wipes. I was also taking up the Jordanian flag, photographs of King Abdullah, Prince Ali and his sister, Princess Haya, the Scottish flag – the Saltire – and, finally, the keffiyeh, the Palestinian scarf.

There was an earlier brief detour, to a mountain village, where I required assistance with a toothache, which resulted in a root filling then extraction without anesthesia! I was suffering terrible pain while I was at Camp 3, acclimatising, so I went to the hospital at base camp, then to the hospital at Namche Bazaar, the so-called 'gateway to Everest', but the dentist had already left for Kathmandu. Then another dentist, Rebecca, from Boston, met me in Namche and in a café took a spoon, looked at my tooth and said grimly, 'It's really bad. Really really bad.' She went to someone who should have given us the key to the dental surgery, but he didn't have it. He said, 'You can break in and pay me $300,' which is what we did.

There were three American dentists in Namche, performing dentistry for local people. I remember Rebecca and her colleagues used old-style X-rays, and then they realised they didn't have sufficient anesthesia but continued regardless. The pain was excruciating and I had to be held down. Actually, I later took the tooth, with a note saying, 'Rebecca – the best dentist in the world,' up Everest.

*

When I got going again, I felt good, and felt strong. In a sense, climbing is relatively easy, and the real challenge is dealing with the altitude. I realised that I wasn't a 'mountaineer', simply someone who enjoyed being on the mountain.

As well as conquering the mountain and reaching the peak, and therefore realising my dream, I also wanted to make the summit on Jordanian Independence Day, which is observed on 25 May every year, to commemorate the day in 1946 when the nation achieved its freedom, when the British command over Jordan ceased. In the back of my mind I remembered that news of the successful 29 May 1953 British Mount Everest expedition, with Edmund Hillary and Tenzing Norgay, reached London in time to be released on the morning of Queen Elizabeth II's coronation. Similarly, I wanted to say a 'thank you' to King Abdullah, Prince Ali and Princess Haya, my sponsors, and to the Jordanian people.

As we were approaching the summit, I made a decision not to spend the night at Camp 4, as we'd initially planned. As previously mentioned, I wanted our possible achievement to coincide with Jordanian Independence Day, and Lakpa agreed to my decision. However, I was suffering frostbite in two toes and thought I might lose them. Reluctantly I shared this information with Lakpa. Startled, he said, 'We have to go back down.' I refused, and said that I was 'happy to lose them, rather than go back.' I was then so determined to keep the blood flowing in my toes that I kept haphazardly kicking my feet on the ground and blood spurted out.

We carried on climbing and passed every team ahead of us. When we got to the Hillary Step at 8,800 metres (28,871 feet) no one else was there. The Hillary Step is a near-vertical rock face, located on the Southeast ridge, and the last real challenge before reaching the top of the mountain via the Southeast route. Ascent and descent of the Hillary Step is generally made with the assistance of fixed ropes, usually placed there by the season's first ascending team. At 8,800 metres oxygen is less than 1 per cent. Essentially the climber has to try and get above a rock, topped by a little snow, and hold on to the right rope, or they are in Tibet or China within a few moments! It takes so much energy and it is also a dangerous climb, because when completed the climber thinks they're at the summit, but there are another 100 metres left.

After the Step we approached the summit. When we were about 20 metres away I stopped and cried like a baby. I thought, 'I've done it.' I thought of all the years I'd tried, the two previous attempts, the training and the endless chasing of sponsorship – it all flashed by. When the sun came out from beneath the clouds I felt like someone had given me ten million dollars, and I felt alive again.

At the summit there was a climber from Denmark, along with his four Sherpas. They soon left. From 6:50 in the morning, for another 40 minutes, we were alone at the top of the world. For a moment I had no real sense of anything, which was not helped by the extreme cold. The top of Everest is not flat, and balance is required. There was no wind. It was silent, peaceful.

I made the *adhan* (call to prayer) and then prayed. Later, still at the summit, I called the king, my mum and dad, and also a woman,

Krissy Gormley, who I would later marry. Lakpa took photographs of me with my various flags and portraits – and a large message on paper stating that I was 'Proud to be a Jordanian' and that I thanked 'all Jordanian people for their support' – and I took some of him. It was Jordanian Independence Day and I had realised my dream. I was above the clouds and all I could see were other peaks.

Strangely enough, at that moment I also remembered what the pioneers had left at the summit in 1953: Tensing buried a bar of chocolate, a packet of biscuits and a few sweets in the snow, as a 'gift to the Gods', and Hillary did the same with a small crucifix. They then planted the Union Jack, the Nepalese national flag and the United Nations flag, ate mint cake and then began their descent.[16]

*

On the way down there were about 100 people on the mountain, and we raced past them all. I felt super, super strong. We went down really quickly, passing the numerous dead bodies left untouched because of the costs involved in removing them. We got to Camp 4 and I asked Lakpa if we could just continue, and again he readily agreed. At Camp 3 we encountered the Alpine Ascent team, and Vern Tejas, who expressed his surprise at our successful climb. In total, I spent 72 days on the climb, including the acclimatisation period.

I had wanted my achievement to coincide with Jordan Independence Day because it celebrates 'freedom and independence' and so is important for Jordanians, and also, of course, tying the climb in with Independence Day would create a greater media impact.

---

[16]See George Craig (2013), *Everest*, London: Carlton.

One of my finest memories of the climb was meeting a team of Iranian mountaineers. We got on very well, and there was mutual respect, despite me being Sunni and they being Shia. On Everest we were just Muslims and human beings. They invited me into their tent, where their meat was halal. They had even constructed a small mosque.

*

On my return to Jordan there was enthusiastic, supportive and exclamatory coverage throughout the media – on television, radio and in print – but I immediately realised there was a problem. Quite simply, the people around the royal family, and perhaps some of the government, were quietly ignoring my achievements because I had embarrassed them by unfurling and then proudly holding the Tibetan flag. This didn't sit well with their geopolitical position.

A short time later, I received the Independence Medal from King Abdullah; I had made a massive contribution to Jordan, put it on the mountaineering map and inspired young Jordanians. The king and I had enjoyed a conversation on the phone when I reached the summit and I had later given him the flag I had taken to the peak. I told him later, when we met, that his phone calls had been a great inspiration for me before I summited Everest and on returning safe and sound to base camp.

*

I left Jordan for Zaragoza in Spain, for some rest and recuperation, and while there saw a doctor who specialised in treating the effects of frostbite. The treatment was paid for by Prince Ali, who was always generous; I will never forget his support. My marriage with Shannon had well and truly ended. We divorced, but not before I had sent

Shannon as much money as I could give her. I went to Scotland and didn't return to America.

*

I partied with 17 friends, all pleased about and proud of my achievement. We stayed up for a few nights – I didn't sleep for four days – and then again I tried to get my life back on track.

On my return to Edinburgh I had started searching for a job and was successful at Hanam's, a Kurdish restaurant near both the Castle and the Royal Mile. I worked predominantly front of house, as a waiter. It was a thriving and busy place, attracting tourist trade and also enormous numbers of Saudi and Qatari students.

Later, I took a job as Head of Catering and Events at Edinburgh Zoo, for something like three months. This was a significant venture, with many corporates hiring the zoo for events, as well as the usual weddings and bar mitzvahs. I loved going into the zoo early in the morning or staying late at night. I liked to sit and watch the sea lion and, better still, the *Suricata suricatta*, more commonly known as meerkats! I wasn't interested in the penguins.

The problem with the job was that I wanted to make certain changes, but the people who worked there had been there 'hundreds of years' and their attitudes and habits simply couldn't be changed.

I moved on to a similar post at the International Festival, but that came to an end when my boss, a friendly and efficient woman, resigned. Her replacement wanted rid of me. He didn't have any issues with my standard of work or ability to manage people, but simply wanted to reduce my salary. Leaving the job didn't disturb me greatly – I never stay where I'm not wanted and am also quite used to conflict. I prefer to move on than endure such conflict – and perhaps I simply don't enjoy working for others.

I didn't want to return to the Sheraton. I was in a strange and confused state of mind, and my spiritual development had again come to a standstill. However, some light emerged in the form of a woman I'd met some four years earlier and whom I'd telephoned from Everest.

I first met Krissy Gormley in 2004, at my best friend, Mark Porter's, wedding. Later, when I reached the summit of Everest in May 2008 I called her on the satellite phone. She must have thought, 'Who is this guy?!' She was asleep and I woke her. I must have sounded like a crazy man. When I returned in August of that year I was talking to Mark's wife, Mary, at another wedding – my friend Simon Dunn's – and she suggested I get in touch with Krissy so we could see each other again.

I'd been interested in Krissy ever since our first meeting. She was athletic and energetic and, unlike most of my close friends, had no interest in drugs. She was very independent. I then started asking her out. I fell in love with her; it was a whirlwind romance and soon we went to the mosque, found two witnesses and married. We were supposed then to sign civil papers but we didn't bother. I knew she wanted a child so I insisted we married.

We moved together to a small but beautiful flat just off Edinburgh's Royal Mile. Then, after I lost the job at the Festival, she said, 'Let's go to Dublin, where I used to teach – I can go back and teach French and German at the same school.' So I agreed, although I was also keen to stay and try to complete the MA I'd started in outdoor studies at the University of Edinburgh. I'd been accepted on the course solely on the basis of my climbing, because usually the requirement was a physical education degree. Once in Dublin I did another personal trainer course and also worked in an outdoors retail shop, selling clothes and equipment. We now have three sons, Ayman, Yacob and Sami James Everest. She has the most amazing heart and is the most caring mother.

*

At this time, Everest and climbing seemed quite some distance away. Then destiny took another turn. Completely out of the blue I received a call from Jordan, from Maher Kaddoura, the founder of the New Think Theatre. Established in 2009, it served as a platform for knowledge and inspiration for the Jordanian community through casual, informal and heart-to-heart dialogue and presentations. New Think Theatre described itself as an organisation that aimed to 'bring on stage people who have a message, something new, to inspire, entertain and above all have a long-lasting impact on the audience' through real-life examples of people who live by such a mantra, innovators in their fields and living examples of thinking outside the box. Maher wanted me to talk about my life, as an example of someone who might act as an inspiration to others. Maher was committed to the idea of inspirational role models and their potential to help others: 'I believe every single human has a giant within him given to him by God. He needs to find it and unleash it.'[17]

Maher invited me to give a presentation, and then a series of one-to-ones, and that opened up a new form of work and a new adventure for me, as I started returning to Jordan more and more. This also enabled me to reacquaint myself with Mary Nazzal-Batayneh, Amman hotel

---

[17]Publicity material, Maher Kaddoura, New Think Theatre.

owner, human rights lawyer and activist for Palestinian rights. I first met Mary through her husband, Aysar, on a flight from the UK to Jordan when he told me that Mary was proud of my achievements, especially given my refugee background. As a result, I met Mary. We agreed on so many issues and strategies, and she gave me money to continue my climbing. Subsequently, both Maher and Mary have become my mentors, and we regularly talk and I seek their advice when I need to make certain decisions.

So once again I began to be 'news' in Jordan. There were numerous articles in newspapers, all along similar lines and asking the question: 'Mostafa Salameh was the first Jordanian to climb Everest. Where is he now, what is he doing?'

From there I started giving motivational talks, lectures and seminars. These would be aimed at school children, college students or, on occasion, Jordanian companies. School children and college students were relatively easy to communicate with, and in my talks I would emphasise leadership and teamwork, but companies were more difficult. To prepare for such events I would read each company's mission statement, set of central values, read the profit and loss sheets, management structure, target market and other such variables, and then design a 'bespoke presentation'. However, the core of all of my talks and lectures, whichever audience I addressed, was that of inspiring people to believe in themselves: 'If you have a dream, you can achieve it. Just look at me.' I would show my audience video clips from my various climbs, recount interesting stories about the highs and lows, and show stills from the top of Everest with me proudly holding the Jordanian flag. I would always conclude this part of my talk with the remark, which I truly believed, that, 'Any of you can climb Mount Everest. The only three things you need are your heart, your mind and your soul.'

I also began to give non-commercial lectures on my background as a refugee, my beliefs and my climbing, and any money raised from these lectures went to support a number of cancer charities. I suggested to Princess Ghida al-Talal, Chairperson of the Trustees Board of the King Hussein Cancer Foundation (KHCF), that I should find people who wanted to pay me to take them on climbs, and who also wanted to raise additional money from sponsorship, and that all such money could be given to charities, especially the King Hussein Cancer Center, in Amman. Princess Ghida had made the centre the finest and most effective in the region. It seemed like a good idea, and in the back of my mind I thought I would take groups of climbers to particular mountains each year, and as a result continuously raise money for good causes. I surmised that with that work and some other part-time work, I'd be able to achieve a reasonable living. I suggested to Princess Ghida a structure as follows: I source a team of people with connections, who can pay for the trip themselves, take 30 per cent of this money as a fee, and, additionally, ensure that each team member raises $50,000 for the charity. This structure, if successful, could change the lives of both the cancer charities' recipients and also the team members who climb for the first time in their lives.

Accordingly, the first climb was to the Everest base camp, and was highly successful, and the second was to Kilimanjaro where I was accompanied by two more Jordanian royals. In a short period of time I raised over $2 million for the King Hussein Cancer Center.

I had further plans as to how to expand these charity climbs, but I encountered problems with the management of the KHCF who, it was suggested, had decided to 'put their own egos before the national interest'. As a consequence of these disagreements, I continued to take climbers annually to Kilimanjaro and to South America, but the proceeds went elsewhere, to UNRWA (the United Nations Relief and Works Agency for Palestine Refugees in the Near East), who were particularly interested in the awareness my climbs would create for the plight of Palestinian refugees. A memorable climb involved me taking a Qatari family to Kilimanjaro: Margarita Zuniga, her son Salman and daughter Sarah. They raised money for breast cancer research in Qatar and climbed on International Cancer Day.

*

Because of my initial sponsorship and support from King Abdullah, and because of my later work for the King Hussein Cancer Trust, I have come to know many of the members of the Jordanian royal family. I admire the king and the queen for the message they are trying to spread to encourage change in Jordan, and the Crown Prince Hussein, who with his youth is having a great impact on young people in Jordan and the Arab world. I also find the king's brother Prince Ali and his wife Princess Reem, and the king's sister, Princess Haya, admirable and honourable, along with Prince Raad Bin Zaid, Prince Talal bin Mohammed and his wife Princess Ghida, who have always been a great support.

7

The Seven Summits & the North Pole

Someone's sitting in the shade today because someone planted
a tree a long time ago.
WARREN BUFFETT

The Orient sought by the mystic, the Orient that cannot be located
on our maps, is in the direction of the north, beyond the north.
HENRY CORBIN

I knew that I could climb, that I had the necessary courage and lack of fear, yet I also knew that it wasn't the passion of my life. But climbing enabled me to raise money for good causes and to highlight issues that consumed me – especially the plight of Palestinian refugees and the injustice of Israel's occupation. So climbing was never far from my mind, and I decided that I should complete the 'Seven Summits' and also attempt to reach both Poles, which would result in massive and widespread publicity for my various causes.

Put simply, the Seven Summits are the highest mountains of each of the seven continents, and the mountaineering challenge of summiting them all was first achieved on 30 April 1985 by Richard Bass, the recently deceased Tulsa-born businessman and climber.

The Seven Summits challenge has become an important goal for climbers around the world and some 325 people have been successful. However, as in most things in mountaineering, there's controversy and dispute, including what constitutes the Seven Summits themselves. From a geological viewpoint, there are only six continents, Africa, Antarctica, Australia, Eurasia, South America and North America, as Europe is considered a peninsula of the Eurasia continental platform and is not a true physical continent. However, from a political perspective, Europe is considered a continent, thus there's an argument that Elbrus (5642 m), located on the border with Asia in southern Russia, represents Europe and not Mont Blanc (4807 m), which lies in the Alps on the border of France and Italy. Then there's the competition between Australia's Kosciuszko (2228 m) and New Guinea's Carstensz Pyramid, also known as Puncak Jaya (4884 m), both located in Oceania, not really a continent but a region of the southwest Pacific that includes Australia, Fiji, New Zealand, Papua New Guinea, Samoa and many other islands.[1] So the list of the Seven Summits is: Aconcagua, Everest, Elbrus or Mont Blanc, Kilimanjaro, Denali, Puncak Jaya or Mount Kosciuszko, and, finally, Vinson.

*

I soon found some sponsors for the last of my Seven Summits, including Duke Mamdouh Bisharat, a cultural philanthropist, archaeology enthusiast and historian who has always treated me like his son, the New Think Theatre and the Landmark Hotel Amman. Having already climbed Aconcagua, Everest, Mont Blanc, Kilimanjaro, Denali and Vinson, I prepared to climb Puncak Jaya,

---

[1] www.alanarnette.com

found in the Sudirman Range of the western central highlands of Papua Province, Indonesia.

Puncak Jaya is one of the more demanding climbs of the Seven Summits, and has the highest technical rating, though the ascent itself doesn't make the greatest physical demands. The standard route to climb the peak from its base camp is up the north face and along the summit ridge, which is a hard rock surface. Despite the large mine alongside, the area is highly inaccessible. The standard route to access base camp is to fly into the nearest major town with an airport, Timika, and then take a small aircraft over the mountain range and on to a makeshift runway at one of the local villages down from the peak. It is then typically a five-day hike to base camp, through very dense jungle and with regular rainfall, making the approach probably the most miserable of the Seven Summits. Rain during most days of the hike inbound and out is not uncommon.

It was indeed very wet and I had no option but to stop in every village. But in these villages I spent enjoyable times, most memorably when I was invited into a hut for some food. I was eating some slightly tough meat and asked what it was: 'That's human flesh; actually it's my mother's arm', was the response. Eating recently deceased relatives was a simple cultural norm for these particular New Guineans.

Climbing Puncak Jaya wasn't easy. In fact, it was exceedingly difficult, as it involved rock climbing, which I wasn't used to. Returning from the peak was also problematic, because I had to take the Dubai-based Palestinian climber Suzanne Al Houby – the first Arab woman to climb Mount Everest – back down with me. She hadn't been able to complete the climb because of altitude problems. Though Suzanne had made it to the summit, on the way back she began to suffer from high altitude sickness which increases through the night. In the morning I decided she needed to be taken down quickly to save her life. On the radio I let people know she was really sick and asked for a helicopter, but one wasn't available. I was then told that the only way back would be through the Grasberg Mine.

The Grasberg Mine is the world's largest gold-mining complex, has over 20,000 employees and is mostly owned by the Freeport-McMoRan Company. The mine continues to work for 24 hours a day, with employees working one of three eight-hour shifts, and has been a frequent source of friction in Papua, because of its environmental impact, the perceived low share of profits going to local Papuans (note that Freeport's annual report shows it made $4.1 billion in operating profit on revenue of $6.4 billion in 2010), and the questionable legality of payments made to Indonesian security forces for their services in guarding the site.[2]

In addition to any problems Suzanne and I might encounter travelling through the mines, there was also the presence of the Indonesian Army and a number of US security firms to consider, but I surmised that as we were both Palestinian Muslims I could be pretty certain the Indonesians wouldn't harm us. So we signed a disclaimer concerning health and safety, listened to all the warnings, and then spent about a day making our way through the mines. This was amazingly quick compared to the ten days we spent walking through the jungle terrain to reach the mountain in the first place.

When we eventually reached the Freeport HQ it was like being in Texas, with numerous burger restaurants and cafés with wi-fi. I rested and just asked for a cigar, of which there were plenty.

*

[2]'Freeport workers protect after killings', *Jakarta Globe*, 8 April 2011.

On my return to Jordan, for once I didn't publicise my Seven Summits achievement. Besides, the media in Jordan follows the king slavishly: essentially, unless the king is involved in a project, no one is interested in anyone's achievements. Again, it is often the people *around* the king, rather than the king himself who influence affairs.

*

In March 2014 I was outraged at the unlawful killing by an Israeli soldier of the 38-year-old Palestinian-Jordanian judge Raed Zeiter, at the Allenby Bridge crossing on the Jordan–Palestine (Israel) border. Angrily, I went on Jordanian television and said that, 'As judges are appointed and protected by the king, and as it states in each Jordanian passport that the king and the army protect the holder, why doesn't the king do something about this outrage?' Of course, the diplomatic, political and strategic issues involved here are based on the fact that Jordan shares with Palestine (Israel) a 365-kilometre (227-mile) border, and therefore wishes to maintain good relations with Israel.

The General Intelligence Directorate, or GID, of Jordan (Dairat al-Mukhabarat al-Ammah), along with the army, is so strong that dissent is barely possible.

*

Owing to its incredible remoteness, the North Pole is sometimes identified in Persian and Sufi literature with a mysterious mountain of ancient Islamic tradition called Mount Qaf (*Jabal Qaf*), the 'farthest point of the earth'.[3] I'd decided, after completing the Seven Summits, that I would mount an expedition to reach the North Pole.

---

[3]Ibrahim Muhawi & Sharif Kanaana (1989), *Speak Bird, Speak Again: Palestinian Arab Folktales*, Berkeley, CA: University of California Press.

My friend and colleague, Dina Shoman, facilitated meetings that resulted in me solving the biggest problem I had with this proposed expedition, namely lack of funding. As a result, I received sponsorship from the telecommunications company Umniah – whose CEO, Ihab Hinnawi, had previously, in 2013, accompanied me on a Climb for Cancer, to Everest base camp – and also from Toyota and Landmark Hotel Amman.

The North Pole, also known as the Geographic North Pole or Terrestrial North Pole, is the point in the Northern Hemisphere where the Earth's axis of rotation meets its surface. It's not to be confused with the North Magnetic Pole. It's the northernmost point on the Earth, lying diametrically opposite the South Pole. At the North Pole all directions point south.

Of course the North Pole is at the centre of profound climatic and geopolitical challenges and changes. As Bruce Parry has remarked, 'It is being transformed from a sea-ice cap to a seasonally ice-free sea…[and]…with the diminishing ice cover, there is new global interest in the extensive energy, shipping, fishing and tourism prospects in the Arctic Ocean.'[4] Russia is not alone as a nuclear-capable state adjusting its strategic deployments in the Arctic. Parry adds that:

The Arctic is now considered the next frontier of hydrocarbon exploration, and although the environmental risks are high, the world's superpowers are eyeing up the region's riches…[and]…the image of a future ice-free Arctic Ocean and the prospects of polar

[4]Bruce Parry (2011), *Arctic*, London: Conway, p. 261.

bears and Inuit peoples struggling in the Far North are at odds with how people perceive this land, and it provokes scientific and public anxiety.[5]

To prepare and train for the expedition, I travelled to France and did some cross-country skiing; I also pulled a sledge with two tyres behind me across the desert-like terrain of Wadi Rum, Jordan; and I did some high-altitude work. I felt I did everything I needed to do.

Any account of the exploration of the North Pole is certain to mention Robert Peary, who, in April 1909, claimed to be the first person in *recorded* history to reach it. He travelled with the aid of dogsleds and three separate support crews, who turned back at successive intervals before reaching the pole. Many modern explorers, including Olympic skiers using modern equipment, contend that Peary could not have reached the pole on foot in the time he claimed.[6] He was also generally vilified, and indeed one polar historian judges him as 'probably the most unpleasant man in the annals of polar exploration'.[7] When Peary left the Arctic, among the things he took with him – including three iron meteorites weighing 37 tons and sacred to Greenlanders – were six Inuit people (described by Peary as 'specimens'), four of whom quickly picked up 'alien germs and died in Washington'.[8]

---

[5]*Ibid.*, p. 261.
[6]'The Arctic', in *Columbia Encyclopedia, Sixth Edition* (2004), New York: Columbia University Press.
[7]See Sara Wheeler (2010), *The Magnetic North*, London: Vintage Books, p. 99.
[8]*Ibid.*, p. 100.

The first consistent, verified, and scientifically convincing attainment of the North Pole was on 12 May 1926, by Norwegian explorer Roald Amundsen and his US sponsor Lincoln Ellsworth, from the airship *Norge*, which was Norwegian-owned but designed and piloted by the Italian Umberto Nobile. The flight started from Svalbard in Norway, and crossed the Arctic Ocean to Alaska. Nobile, with several scientists and crew from the *Norge*, overflew the pole a second time on 24 May 1928, in the airship *Italia*, which crashed on its return with the loss of half its crew.[9]

*

The expedition I was part of, in 2014, was far from easy. I'd previously been in Antarctica, so of course I had experience of the extreme cold weather I would encounter. We set off from north Norway, from Longyearbyen, in the Svalbard archipelago, and then were flown to the Russian drifting station somewhere in Siberia, the starting point of the expedition. Thereafter we had to walk two weeks to the pole.

Informally, and reluctantly at first, I took on the role of guide, but soon enjoyed taking care of my teammates, cooking, and keeping their morale up. I was looking after two people in my tent, motivating them and explaining the finer details of the planned route. Our particular route was the 'last degree', where we would ski the final 100 kilometres (62 miles) from the 89th parallel to the North Pole.

The 'land' upon which we walked is frozen open water. It made me think, 'Yes, there's climate warming, but surely this will take hundreds

---

[9]John Tierney, 'Who was first at the North Pole?', *New York Times*, 7 September 2009.

if not thousands of years to occur?' We were constantly walking, on some days for ten hours or longer, and inside the tent the air was cold and wet. It was absolutely freezing.

There was an Israeli in the party, who at first made me feel slightly uneasy, given my background and my connections to the BDS movement (Boycott, Divestment and Sanctions). However, on reflection I realise my initial reaction was perhaps rather adolescent and, ultimately, I'm pleased to say I was able to put the expedition first.

So, we walked for two weeks and it was always cold. Twenty-four-hours-a-day cold. It was cold outside the tent, cold inside the tent. It was absolutely miserable. I did most of the work and helped the two guys in the tent, where we spent the time constantly talking. I was with another English guy, Alan, who invested in companies and who simply wanted to complete the journey, and a remarkable Chinese man, Fey, who was a teacher, and liked big adventures; he was constantly trying to learn about Islam, and wanted to perform the *salat* (prayer). Meanwhile, I did all the cooking, which I thoroughly enjoyed. I lived for the moment. Loved it. I learned so much, for example, about what was involved in sustained skiing.

While walking, I would constantly talk to myself. I found my thoughts interesting: I designed and constructed numerous projects and expeditions, and any of these projects and plans that entered my mind I believed were possible to achieve. I would also recite the Qur'an, and when in the tent would read verses that were precious to me. I listened to music. In the morning it would always be Nina Simone, followed by a small amount of Arabic music, at midday some techno, then in the evening I would try and relax with Vivaldi or Beethoven. It was, however, never easy to sleep. It was always so cold and wet!

We reached the North Pole, at 90 degrees. We shook hands and man-hugged, I prayed, then we took the obligatory photographs and waited for the helicopter to winch us to safety and onwards to the journey home.

*

Whenever I address an audience, I'm always asked the question, 'What's the point of exploring or mountaineering?' For me, the answer is highly personal. If it weren't for my Edinburgh dream I'd never have set foot on any mountain anywhere on the globe or explored any distant land or terrain.

I've climbed for causes, especially for cancer relief and for Palestinians and the children of Gaza. There's a mystique to mountaineering which, I believe, is to a great degree somewhat unfounded. Anyone can climb mountains. For example, if someone has the finance, a good guide, a Sherpa or two, Everest can be conquered.

*

In 2015, my expedition 'Climb for the Children of Gaza', organised with the great help of Ruba Atallah, a dear friend and a great person, took me and my chosen team members to Peru and Bolivia. We raised a lot of money for UNRWA and then, as always, it felt good to raise funds for Palestinian refugees. The team was amazing. For example, there was Zeena Kalaldeh, a Jordanian interested in Sufism, then there was Zein Salti, a yoga teacher who I'd known since she was 12 years old, when I'd remarked to her that one day she'd travel with me, and she has – Everest base camp, Kilimanjaro, and then Peru and Bolivia. And, last but certainly not least, there was Hanna Khoury, a huge man who'd trained hard and lost some of his immense weight for the climb – and, sweating and panting, managed to climb all 500 steps of the Inca sanctuary of Machu Picchu.

*

In 2015, there was also an adventure I undertook called 'See No Limits', where I climbed Kilimanjaro with two less-able men. We sought to deliver messages which included one asserting that Islam was a religion of peace and another that 'nothing is impossible'. My two companions were Jordanian men, one with a visual disability and the other an amputee.

Suhail Nashash, 31, who lost his eyesight aged 16 following a 'medical error' which involved an overdose of cortisone medication, participated in 'See No Limits' in an attempt to deliver the message that people with visual disabilities are not different, and to show that he could climb Kilimanjaro just as an able-bodied person could. I first met Suhail in 2012, when I had this idea in my head that it would be good to take a blind guy to the highest point in Jordan. We met, got on well, and then together climbed Jebel Um Adaami – at 1,800 metres (5,905 feet) the highest peak in the country. I then asked him, 'Would you like to climb Kilimanjaro?' and he enthusiastically agreed.

At the launch of the initiative, held at the Landmark Hotel Amman, he told an interviewer from the *Jordan Times* that 'we also want to show the world that Islam is a religion of peace, love and moderation, and that it encourages achievements and the appreciation of life'. A professional athlete and winner of several gold medals in local, regional and international marathons, Suhail said he hoped his participation might change the world's perceptions: 'When I became blind, I lost hope in life, but after a while and with hard work I returned to my normal life. Nothing is impossible with determination and hard work.'

Then, some time later, I was talking to someone at a charity event who told me about an athlete with a prosthetic leg who also possessed an adventurous spirit. Jarrah Hawamdeh was diagnosed with a tumour in his right leg, subsequently had an amputation from the hip, and at the age of 19 began a new life with a prosthetic. He told the *Jordan Times* that his participation in 'See No Limits' was intended to offer hope to cancer patients and also to show that nothing is impossible.

Once in Africa, we had interesting times together but, sadly, only Suhail made it to the top of Kilimanjaro. Jarrah, meanwhile, remained at base camp. On a positive note, we raised all the money we'd hoped for and I believe that all three of us benefited from the experience, as did the African porters who helped us and who were surprised that such men as Suhail and Jarrah were attempting the climb in the first place!

The reason why Jarrah didn't succeed was that, essentially, he wasn't listening to me or taking any notice of my technical advice. In particular, he was unadvisedly taking morphine, to alleviate pain, when he shouldn't have. Quite simply, at 5,000 metres (16,404 feet), it shouldn't be taken. When leading any climb I have to know about any medication a climber is taking: in Jarrah's case, without prior knowledge of this medication I wouldn't be able to wake him up should he lose consciousness due to the altitude or effects of the drug. But, sadly, he thought he knew everything and ignored my protestations.

Suhail only possesses a two-year passport from Jordan because he's originally from Gaza. Technically it's not actually a passport, more a travel document. The injustice is that, for example, the Jordanian government give applicants from Iraq passports, because they contribute so much money to the Jordanian economy. Suhail is a sports champion representing Jordan and one of its main hopes at the next Paralympics. He worked for Zain Telecommunications and was quite a role model, yet the company threatened to sack him if I held an Umniah flag or logo on the summit, for Umniah are their competitor. I couldn't believe it: the fact that the manager of a major company felt the need to threaten a blind man trying to do good.

After Suhail had become the first blind Muslim to climb Kilimanjaro, we left Africa for Qatar. And there Suhail's travails continued: I held a British passport and could be booked into a five-star hotel, Jarrah could be booked into a three-star hotel, because of his Jordanian passport, but Suhail, because of the papers he held and his lack of a proper passport, was simply left in an airport lounge for 17 hours. I spoke with the immigration officials, told them of his achievements and the fact that he was blind, and they still left him there.

8

Islam

Beyond what we wish and what we fear may happen, we have another life…as clear and free as a mountain stream.
JALĀL AD-DĪN MUHAMMAD RŪMĪ

What does a man seek in this world? A position or a throne? Man seeks peace of mind and the fear of almighty God as long as one knows that there's a judgement day, he tries to keep his conscience clear and do what he can.
KING HUSSEIN I

In his history of nineteenth-century exploration of the North Pole, Fergus Fleming observes that, 'like those who have been to the moon, North Polar explorers seem to have been marked permanently by the experience', and that on their return they often 'succumbed to a malaise of indifference and at times depression'.[1] Whether it's because modern expeditions are that much easier, with better equipment and navigation and with prior knowledge, or whether I have a different personality, I don't know, but I felt no indifference or depression on my

---

[1]Fergus Fleming (2001), *Ninety Degrees North: The Quest for the North Pole*, London: Granta Books, p. 419.

return from the North Pole. Instead, I was planning future climbs and adventures, and thinking more and more about Palestine, Sufism and Islam, the religion of my birth. Whether it was because of the anger I felt meeting the Israeli on the expedition, or whether it was simply the long periods of time spent walking, when my mind focused and concentrated in order to keep out the cold, I returned and decided to ensure that I would continue to spread the message of peaceful Islam.

*

A day doesn't pass without Islam making headlines worldwide, on television, radio, in newspapers and, increasingly, on the Internet. Coverage includes reports of governments attempting to ban Islamic dress; reports of preachers and their teaching of *jihad*; stories of the various tragedies faced by refugee migrants from the Middle East; Christians complaining that Muslims are allowed to celebrate their faith when they themselves can't; headlines about so-called 'Islamic terror', with reports of attacks on homosexuals, women, innocent civilians and combatants; and, finally, reportage of the seemingly relentless rise of so-called 'Islamic State'.

As a result, Islam is blamed for much of this global mayhem and disorder, whether through so-called 'jihadi' groups or individuals acting, allegedly, on behalf of Islam.

This is just wrong and plain stupid.

*

I met a woman called Carolyn Newton at the airport in Amman who would become one of my best friends. We hit it off and talked about everything under the sun, but mostly spiritual matters. We still talk, and, importantly, she introduced me to a book, *The Case for God*, by

Karen Armstrong. I have often turned to Armstrong's writings, in her books and journalism, and have found her ideas to be both agreeable and thought-provoking.

In her discussion of so-called 'terrorists', she argues that they have very little knowledge of the Qur'an, and she argues that it is pointless to attempt a discussion about the interpretation of scripture or to blame 'Islam' for their crimes. She adds that, 'Indeed, Marc Sageman, who has talked with several of them, believes that a "normal religious education might have deterred them from their crimes"'; rather, she continues, they appear to be 'chiefly motivated by the desire to escape a stifling sense of insignificance and pointlessness in secular nation states that struggle to absorb foreign minorities'. And, as a result, they seek the 'age-old dream of military glory and believe that by dying a heroic death they will give their lives meaning as local heroes… [and]…they may claim to be acting in the name of Islam, but when an untalented beginner claims to be playing a Beethoven sonata, we hear only cacophony'.[2] Quite simply, these individuals have neither the basis nor the right to claim that their heinous and murderous actions are based on the Qur'an in particular or Islam in general.

Armstrong, a former Roman Catholic nun and leading commentator on world religion, also discusses another side to this contemporary scenario, namely the understated and under-reported facts about the West's contribution – either in the form of illegal wars or the attacks on civilians (sometimes sickeningly known as 'collateral damage') – to Islamic or ersatz Islamic anger and disquiet. She tells

---

[2]Karen Armstrong (2014), *Fields of Blood: Religion and the History of Violence*, London: The Bodley Head, p. 357. Armstrong quotes Marc Sageman, (2008), *Leaderless Jihad*, Philadelphia, PA: University of Pennsylvania Press, pp. 156–57.

the story of Mamana Bibi, a 68-year-old woman who, on 24 October 2012, was quietly and leisurely picking vegetables on her family's large, open land in northern Waziristan, Pakistan, when a United States drone aircraft killed her:

> She was not a terrorist but a midwife married to a retired schoolteacher, yet she was blown to pieces in front of her nine grandchildren. Some of the children have had multiple surgeries that the family could ill afford because they lost all their livestock; the smaller children still scream in terror all night long. We do not know who the real targets were…[but]…the US government has never apologised, never offered compensation to the family, nor even admitted to the American people what happened.[3]

Of course there have been many more similar deaths of innocent civilians, as organisations like Amnesty International frequently report, yet no one in the West appears to care greatly. The result is that it creates hatred in the hearts of hitherto peaceful people.

Armstrong is one among many commentators who point to the West's contribution to this age of chaos. Raja Shehadeh recalls the day that former French Prime Minister Dominique de Villepin (who led the opposition to the Iraq War) spoke on BFM TV in the wake of the January 2015 *Charlie Hebdo* attacks in France and described the so-called Islamic State as the 'deformed child' of Western policy. The former prime minister also wrote in *Le Monde* that the West's wars in the Middle East 'nourish terrorism among us with promises of eradicating it'.[4]

---

[3]*Ibid.*, p. 358.
[4]Shehadeh (2014), p. 247.

*

In 2015 the UK charity Islamic Relief commissioned a YouGov poll to elicit British views about Islam. First of all, they asked respondents to name the three words they associate with the term 'Muslim' and found that more think of 'terror/terrorism/terrorist' (12 per cent) than 'faith' (11 per cent) or 'Koran' (Qur'an) (8 per cent). Levels of awareness around Ramadan appeared to be slightly higher, with an overwhelming majority of the 6,600 respondents recognising it as a holy month for Muslims, although, worryingly, 15 people thought it was a variety of nut from South America and 24 thought it was an endangered species of amphibian.

Islamic Relief's UK director, Jehangir Malik, said the results of the survey were 'extremely worrying' because they show that 'public attitudes towards Muslims are hugely negative'.[5] Despite the fact that my major spiritual practice is Sufism and that I embrace many other spiritual traditions and psychological techniques concerned with self-awareness and motivation, it is Islam that centres me. Islam is the core of my faith in Allah, a faith that gives me freedom to act without fear of death and uncertainty. It therefore pains me when I have to endure the gross ignorance and negativity that surrounds Islam.

*

On 5 February 2012, when Newcastle United played Aston Villa at St James's Park, one moment symbolised the impact Muslim players were having on the Premier League. After 30 minutes, Demba Ba scored for the home side, raced to the corner flag and was joined by

---

[5]Press release, Islamic Relief, 2015.

Senegalese compatriot Papiss Cissé. The two devout Muslims then sank to their knees in prayer.

Over the past decade, young men with origins in remote villages of West Africa or tough estates in Paris have become global soccer stars. Although many have found wealth and fame, many still hold on to their cultural identity, something that guides them and comforts them, namely their Islamic faith. When a player of Ba's calibre says he's serious about his faith, clubs should listen. And indeed there is a genuine willingness on the part of clubs to understand and accommodate the religious needs of their players. So, for example, Muslim footballers are provided with halal food, have the option to shower separately from the rest of the team, and are given time and space for prayer.

Yet there are challenges to managing Muslim players and Ramadan is a good example. How can players who aren't eating or drinking for 18 hours a day perform at the highest level? Some players insist on fasting every day, others may fast during training but not on a match day, and as a consequence clubs tend to muddle through with some kind of compromise.

It saddens me that so many people appear unable to understand that Muslims come in so many different colours, shapes and sizes, with varied personalities, skills and occupations, talents and achievements. Consider the following perfunctory list of well-known individuals: Asim Shahmalak, transplant surgeon who, in 2009, performed the UK's first eyelash transplant; Richard Thompson, singer and musician, Sufi and Muslim; Iman, fashion model married to David Bowie; Haroon Ahmed, prominent scientist in the fields of microelectronics and electrical engineering; Rozina Ali, microvascular reconstructive plastic surgeon; rapper Ice Cube; Jemima Khan, born Jewish but converted when married to Imran Khan, now divorced but still a Muslim; Sheraz Daya, ophthalmologist and eye surgeon, best known for his founding of the Centre for Sight in 1996 and his work in the use of stem-cell research during sight recovery surgery; Shaquille O'Neal, retired American professional basketball player; the late, great Qawwali singer, Nusrat Fateh Ali Khan; Yusuf Islam, the singer previously known as Cat Stevens; Charlie Parker, the legendary saxophonist; Malcolm X; Amal Clooney, human rights lawyer.

*

Mahmoud Hussein asks the question, 'Can one find a Qur'anic reference to the actions of those kamikazes who blow themselves up in a public space or on the underground, indiscriminately killing combatants and civilians, young and old?'[6] He answers his own question by pointing to verse 5:32, in which a person is condemned if they take the life of an innocent person: 'The Prophet forbade Muslims to kill themselves, and permitted them to kill only armed and adult enemy combatants, excluding women, old people and children.'[7] Hussein then poses another question: 'How can certain Muslims nevertheless commit such crimes?' and again he states that such aggressors cite verse (9:3–5) which calls for combat against the idolaters, and then describes as such all those whom they consider to be their enemies. In other words, 'they make the Qur'an say what suits them'.[8]

---

[6]Mahmoud Hussein (2013), *Understanding the Qur'an Today*, London: Saqi Books, p. 10.
[7]*Ibid.*
[8]*Ibid.*

Muslims use the word *jihad* to describe different kinds of struggle: a believer's internal struggle to live out the Muslim faith as successfully as possible, and the struggle to defend Islam, with force if necessary (also known as the Holy War).

The internal *jihad* is the one that Prophet Muhammad is said to have called the *greater jihad*, so Muslims make a great effort to live as Allah has instructed, following the rules of the faith and doing everything they can to help other people. For most people, living Allah's way is in itself quite a struggle, as Allah sets high standards and believers have to fight with their own selfish desires to live up to them, no matter how much they love Allah.

The Five Pillars of Islam form an exercise of *jihad* in this sense, since a Muslim gets closer to Allah by performing them. Other ways in which a Muslim engages in the *greater jihad* could include learning the Qur'an by heart, or overcoming feelings such as anger, greed, hatred, pride or malice, or working for social justice, and so on.

On his return from a battle, the Prophet said, 'We are finished with the lesser jihad; now we are starting the greater jihad.'[9] He explained to his followers that fighting against an outer enemy is the *lesser jihad* and fighting against one's self is the *greater jihad*. This quotation has been very influential among some Muslims, and Sufis in particular.

When Muslims, or their faith or territory, are under attack, Islam allows the believer to wage military war to protect them. However, Islamic (*sharia*) law sets very strict rules for the conduct of such a war.

---

[9]This section has relied considerably on the BBC's religious webpages, www.wikipedia.org, and a number of standard textbooks.

The Qur'an is clear that self-defence is always the underlying cause, but in addition the following may also be accepted as justification: strengthening Islam, protecting the freedom of Muslims to practise their faith, protecting Muslims against oppression and overthrowing a tyrannical ruler.

Conversely, a war is not a *jihad* if the intention is to force people to convert to Islam, or to conquer or attempt to colonise nations, take territory for economic gain, settle disputes or demonstrate a leader's power. Although the Prophet engaged in military action on a number of occasions, these were battles to survive, and took place at a time when fighting between tribes was common. *Jihad* must be launched by a religious leader; must be fought to bring about good, that is to say, something that Allah will approve of; every other way of solving the problem must have been attempted; innocent people, women, children or old people, should not be killed or injured; women should not be raped; enemies must be treated with justice; wounded enemy soldiers must be treated in exactly the same way as one's own soldiers; the war must stop as soon as the enemy asks for peace; property must not be damaged; and 'poisoning wells is forbidden', the earlier version of chemical or biological warfare.

My religion consists of a number of core beliefs: the belief in Allah as the one and only God; belief in angels; belief in all the holy books; belief in all the prophets, Adam, Ibrahim (Abraham), Musa (Moses), Dawud (David), Isa (Jesus); the belief that Muhammad is the final prophet; belief in the Day of Judgement (the day when the life of every human being will be assessed to decide whether they go to heaven or hell); and belief in predestination. It's important to note that although at the heart of faith for all Muslims is obedience to Allah's will, this does not stop human beings making free choices. Allah is eternal, omniscient and omnipotent, has always existed and will always exist, knows everything that can be known, can do anything that can be done, has no shape or form, can't be seen or heard, is neither male or female, is just and rewards and punishes fairly, and is *merciful*.

*

Whenever I witness the various flashpoints centred on images of the Prophet, such as the insulting *Jyllands-Posten* cartoons in Denmark, the *Charlie Hebdo* cartoons, the various activities of Dutch extremist Geert Wilders and many others, and *then* witness the outpourings of sympathy for many of these perpetrators, I wonder what the general public actually knows of the Prophet.

Muhammad ibn 'Abd Allah ibn 'Abd al-Muttalib (*ṣalla llāhu 'alayhi wa-alehe wa-sallam*) was born in Makkah, in the year 570, in the 'prestigious yet impoverished clan of the Banu 'Abd al-Muttalib, traditional guardians of the sanctuary of the Kaaba'.[10] He grew up an orphan, with his father's death shortly before his birth followed by the death of his mother when he was only six years old. He was then looked after by his grandfather, and throughout his infant and adolescent years his life was one of relative poverty. Little is known about the first 40 years of his life, perhaps with the exception that he always favoured solitude, sought out the company of learned people, and appeared to possess an upright and honest personality. At the age of 25 he married Khadija, a wealthy businesswoman who was 15 years older than him. She remained his only wife until her death.

---

[10]Hussein (2013), p. 29.

Around the year 610, on the seventeenth night of Ramadan, the Prophet was meditating in a cave named Hira, near Makkah, when he learned that Allah had chosen him as his final messenger. He believed that the angel Gabriel had appeared before him and uttered the command, 'Recite!' Muhammad was illiterate, yet the first sentence of the Qur'an came from his lips. Throughout his life, Muhammad continued to receive 'intermittently the Word of God'.[11] Muhammad was often left exhausted, shivering with cold and covered with a blanket. He would slump with his head between his knees when a revelation came to him.

In the year 630, the Prophet Muhammad achieved one of his most cherished goals: the conquest of Makkah and the subsequent cleansing of the city from idol worship. It was a political and religious victory of immense symbolic importance. Makkah had been declared the centre of the new faith, so its conquest was therefore the fulfilment of a divine promise. Entering the Ka'aba, the square structure that housed the city's idols, Muhammad ordered that all its icons be cleansed or destroyed. One of the icons in what must have been a very mixed gallery of divinities was a Virgin and child. Muhammad covered it with his cloak and ordered that all the others be washed away. Islam's preoccupation with Jesus may well be unique among the world's great non-Christian religions.

There are 114 chapters in the Qur'an, and all except one begin with the sentence *Bismillahir rahmanir raheem*: 'In the name of Allah the most merciful and the most kind'. This is the thought with

---

[11]*Ibid.*, p. 30.

which Muslims should start every action. The Qur'an is sometimes divided into 30 roughly equal parts, and these divisions make it easier for Muslims to read the Qur'an during the course of a month; many will read one each day, particularly during Ramadan. Translations of the Qur'an exist in over 40 languages but Muslims are still taught to learn and recite it in Arabic, even if this is not their native language. At the time of the revelation of the Qur'an, books were not readily available and so it was common for people to learn it by heart. Committing the Qur'an to memory acted as a great aid for its preservation, and any person who is able to accomplish this is known as a *hafiz*.

Other sacred sources are the *Sunnah*, the example set by the Prophet, and the *Hadith*, reports of what the Prophet Muhammad said or approved.

*

Sharia law is a term familiar to both Muslims and non-Muslims. It can often be heard in news stories about politics, crime, feminism, terrorism and civilisation. All aspects of a Muslim's life are governed by *Sharia*.

Sharia law comes from a combination of sources including the Qur'an, the *Hadith* and *fatwas* (the rulings of Islamic scholars). Many people, including Muslims, misunderstand *Sharia*. It's often associated with the amputation of limbs, or death by stoning, lashes and other medieval punishments, and because of this, it's sometimes thought of as draconian. However, in the Islamic tradition *Sharia* is seen as something divinely revealed, and in a society where social problems are widespread, *Sharia* frees humanity to realise its individual potential.

In Arabic, *Sharia* means 'the clear, well-trodden path to water', and its linguistic meaning reverberates in its technical usage: just as water is vital to human life, so the clarity and uprightness of *Sharia* is the means of life for souls and minds.

The whole principle of God's will is to bring about compassion, kindness, generosity, justice, fair play, tolerance and care in general, as opposed to tyranny, cruelty, selfishness, and exploitation. All the rules of *Sharia* are towards those ends.

The usual criticisms of *Sharia* – that it is cruel as regards execution, flogging and cutting off hands, etc. – totally ignore all the extenuating circumstances that would lead to these penalties *not* being applied. The cutting off of the hand for theft is a very powerful deterrent – Muslims care less for the callous and continual thief than they do for the poor souls who are mugged and robbed and hurt by the thieves. The Middle East is certainly not full of one-handed people. Muslims believe that Allah sees every single thing that's done, there are no secrets. Even if you get away with something on earth, it's been seen and recorded and you will have to face judgement for it eventually, and the people hurt by your action will be recompensed. Of course, if you don't believe in Allah, or a judgement, or a life to come, the whole system is quite meaningless. In *Sharia* law, if a thief could prove that he/she only stole because of need, then the Muslim society would be held at fault and made to supply that need, and there would be no hand-cutting.

When I walk along the streets of Dublin, London, Edinburgh – and certainly Luton, when I visit Mazen – I see more and more women wearing burqas. Thankfully, unlike in France and the Netherlands, the UK and Ireland have not resorted to draconian laws to restrict their use. This is another area of misunderstanding.

Sharia law does not require women to wear a burqa. There are all sorts of items of dress that are worn by Muslim women, and these vary all over the world. Burqas belong to particular areas of the world, where they are considered normal dress. In other parts of the world the dress is totally different. The rule of dress for women is *modesty*, and the word hijab implies 'covered'. When men try to enforce Muslim dress on women, this is forbidden; no aspect of my faith is to be enforced by coercion.

In *Sharia* law any marriage that is forced or false in any way is, as a consequence, null and void. It is not a proper marriage. This is a problem that seems to plague Muslim women from India, Pakistan and Bangladesh, and nowhere else in the Islamic world – and it also applies to Hindus and some Sikhs from those regions. Forced marriage is totally forbidden in Islam. False marriage is, too – for example, some of our teenage girls are sent back to Pakistan for a holiday when they are about 15, and sign things they do not understand, and then find out later that they have been 'married' even if it has not been consummated.

*

The words Sunni and Shia appear regularly in stories about the Muslim world but few people know what they really mean. This division is the largest and oldest in the history of Islam. Both sects agree on the fundamentals of Islam, but there are differences mostly derived from their different historical experiences, political and social developments, as well as ethnic composition. These differences originate from the question of who would succeed the Prophet Muhammad as leader of the emerging Muslim community after his death in the early seventh century. He left behind not only the religion of Islam but also a community of about one hundred thousand Muslims organised as an Islamic state on the Arabian Peninsula. It was the question of who should succeed the Prophet and lead the fledgling Islamic state that created the divide.

The larger group of Muslims chose Abu Bakr, a close Companion of the Prophet, as the Caliph (politico-social leader) and he was accepted by much of the community, which saw the succession in political and not spiritual terms. However another smaller group, which also included some of the senior Companions, believed that the Prophet's son-in-law and cousin, Ali, should be Caliph. They understood that the Prophet had appointed him as the sole interpreter of his legacy, in both political and spiritual terms. In the end Abu Bakr was appointed First Caliph.

Both Shias and Sunnis have good evidence to support their understanding of the succession. Sunnis argue that the Prophet chose Abu Bakr to lead the congregational prayers as he lay on his deathbed, thus suggesting that the Prophet was naming Abu Bakr as the next leader. The Shias' evidence is that Muhammad stood up in front of his Companions on the way back from his last *hajj* and proclaimed Ali the spiritual guide and master of all believers. Shia reports say he took Ali's hand and said that anyone who followed Muhammad should follow Ali.

Sunni means 'one who follows the Sunnah' (what the Prophet said, did, agreed to or condemned). Shia is a contraction of the phrase 'Shiat Ali', meaning 'partisans of Ali'.

Both agree that Muhammad was the final prophet.

Significant numbers of Shias are now found in many countries including Iraq, Pakistan, Albania and Yemen, and they constitute

90 per cent of the population of Iran, which is the contemporary political face of *Shia* Islam.

Initially the difference between Sunni and Shia was merely a question of who should lead the Muslim community. As time went on, however, the Shia began to show a preference for particular *Hadith* and *Sunnah* literature. Ultimately this difference of emphasis led to different understandings of the laws and practices of Islam.

The Wahhabi movement within Sunni Islam views the Shia practice of visiting and venerating shrines to the imams of the Prophet's family and other saints and scholars as heretical, but most mainstream Sunni Muslims have no objections. Some Sufi movements, which often provide a bridge between Shia and Sunni theologies, help to unite Muslims of both traditions and encourage visiting and venerating these shrines.

As the Sunni Ottoman Empire expanded into the Balkans and central Asia, and the Shia Safavid dynasty spread through the Persian Empire from the sixteenth century, tensions arose in Sunni–Shia relations. However, the majority of contemporary Sunni and Shia Muslims do not allow their theological differences to divide them or cause hostility between them. Current global political conditions mean there has been a degree of polarisation and hostility in many Muslim societies. The term Rafidi (meaning 'rejecter') has been applied by radical Sunnis to disparage Shias. In turn the Shias will often use the label Wahhabi as a term of abuse for all those who disagree with Shia beliefs and practices.

*

One of those many autobiographies I devoured, trying to gain insights into motivation and leadership and single-mindedness, was of the philosopher, mathematician and chemist Abu Bakr Mohammad Ibn Zakariya al-Razi (854–925 AD). On reading about him I was struck by the remark attributed to him that the 'birth of genius is the moment that the human discovers his talent, and you should follow it no matter how old you are'.

This polymath was initially influenced by Hippocrates, and subsequently wrote numerous books on a wide range of medical and scientific subjects. The *Al-Mansuri* and *Al-Hawi*, his encyclopedic reviews of medicine, were translated into several languages and for centuries became standard texts for Islamic and even European medical students. He saw the importance of recording a patient's case history and made clinical notes about the progress and symptoms of different illnesses, including his own. One of his early findings was that measles and smallpox were different diseases, not the same. But al-Razi also wrote controversially about religion, and in this area of his thought and scholarship his legacy has been fiercely contested. According to some commentators, Razi offered harsh criticism concerning religions, in particular those religions that claim to have been revealed by prophetic experiences.[12] Indeed, it's believed that al-Razi asked a question that might be seen as a direct criticism of Islam, the religion he was born into: 'On what ground do you deem it necessary that God should single out certain individuals by giving them prophecy, that he should set them up above other people, that he should appoint them to be the people's guides, and make people dependent upon them?'[13]

---

[12]This section relies heavily on www.wikipedia.org and Jennifer Michael Hecht (2003), *Doubt: A History: The Great Doubters and Their Legacy of Innovation, from Socrates and Jesus to Thomas Jefferson and Emily Dickinson*, San Francisco, CA: Harper, pp. 227–30
[13]*Ibid.*, p. 230.

He was also critical of the lack of interest among religious believers in the rational analysis of their beliefs and why truth becomes 'thoroughly silenced and concealed',[14] and of those who kill their adversaries. He believed that so-called common people had originally been duped into belief by religious authority figures and by the status quo. He further believed that the existence of a large variety of religions was, in itself, evidence that they were all *man-made* and, from the beginning of human history, all of those who claimed to be prophets were possibly devious or psychologically unwell.

There are innumerable accounts and interpretations of al-Razi's work and beliefs, and there are innumerable contradictory arguments *within* his work. However, I was engaged by his determination to speak out, at a dangerous historical time, to be unafraid of expressing his opinions, however unpopular they might be.

It is in this spirit that I embrace the religion of my birth. Some Sunnis are extremists, some Shia are extremists. But others are not, and people are people. For example, I am Sunni, yet I have great admiration for Iran, which has gained so much respect from the world because of its power and its 2015 deal with the USA, which will result in the reduction of Saudi influence. Iran achieved its momentous deal because it is powerful, not weak.

---

[14]*Ibid.*

9

Palestine, Isis, Radicalisation

*If any one killed a person, it would be as if he killed the
whole of mankind; and if any one saved a life, it would be
as if he saved the life of the whole of mankind.*

QUR'AN, 5:32

*I remember how it was in 1948 when Israel was being established
and all my Jewish friends were ecstatic; I was not. I said:
what are we doing? We are establishing ourselves in a ghetto,
in a small corner of a vast Muslim sea. The Muslims
will never forget nor forgive, and Israel, as long as
it exists, will be embattled.*

ISAAC ASIMOV

I was sitting in the departure lounge at Queen Alia International Airport, Amman, waiting for a flight to Doha, Qatar. I picked up a newspaper and once again was utterly captivated by the brilliance and wisdom of English writer and journalist Robert Fisk. For many years I have turned to him when wanting to read an English-language account of the latest Middle Eastern tragedy. In this particular piece, written in May 2015, he describes the bewildering chaos unfolding before us all. He writes with a sense of incredulity, under the title 'Who is bombing whom in the Middle East?',[1] and wonders whether he has the details correct. The 'Saudis are bombing Yemen because they fear the Shia Houthis are working for the Iranians. The Saudis are also bombing Isis in Iraq and Isis in Syria. So are the United Arab Emirates', and he continues to add that the 'Syrian government is bombing its enemies in Syria and the Iraqi government is also bombing its enemies in Iraq. America, France, Britain, Denmark, Holland, Australia and – believe it or not – Canada are bombing Isis in Syria and Isis in Iraq, partly on behalf of the Iraqi government (for which read Shia militias) but absolutely not on behalf of the Syrian government'. And it doesn't end there, as Fisk continues to point out that the 'Jordanians and Saudis and Bahrainis are also bombing Isis in Syria and Iraq because they don't like them, but the Jordanians are bombing Isis even more than the Saudis after their pilot-prisoner was burned to death in a cage', and, in a similar vein, the 'Egyptians are bombing parts of Libya because a group of Christian Egyptians had their heads chopped off by what might – notionally – be the same so-called Islamic State, as Isis refers to itself. The Iranians have acknowledged bombing Isis in Iraq – of which the Americans (but not the Iraqi government) take a rather dim view'. And he concludes by adding that, of course, the Israelis have several times bombed Syrian government forces in Syria but not Isis.[2]

Fisk captures the madness of all this when he adds that he's amazed that all 'these warriors of the air don't regularly crash into each other as they go on bombing and bombing'. The Sunni Saudis are bombing

[1]Robert Fisk, 'Who is bombing whom in the Middle East?', *Independent*, 4 May 2015.
[2]*Ibid.*

the Shia Yemenis and the Shia Iranians are bombing the Sunni Iraqis. The Sunni Egyptians are bombing Sunni Libyans, and the Jordanian Sunnis are bombing Iraqi Sunnis. But the Shia-supported Syrian government forces are bombing their Sunni Syrian enemies and the Lebanese Hezbollah – Shia to a man – are fighting Syrian President Bashar al-Assad's Sunni enemies, along with Iranian Revolutionary Guards and an ever-larger number of Afghan Shia men in Syrian uniforms. On a serious note, he points to the sectarianism of all this, and reports that Saudi Arabia's latest request for more Pakistani troops to protect the kingdom (and possibly help to invade Yemen) included an outrageous second request, namely that the Pakistanis send only Sunni Muslim soldiers and that Pakistani Shia Muslim men would not be welcome. Fisk recalls the fact that Pakistani soldiers were killed by the Iraqi army in the battle for the Saudi town of Khafji in 1991, and they weren't all Sunnis.

Fisk concludes his thought-provoking piece on the often forgotten destructive force in this chaos, namely the arms trade, or, as he puts it, 'the really big winners in all this blood, the weapons manufacturers'.[3] Indeed, in 2014, Raytheon and Lockheed Martin supplied £1.3 billion of missiles to the Saudis. But three years ago, in 2012, *Der Spiegel* claimed the European Union was Saudi Arabia's most important arms supplier and in the summer of 2015 France announced the sale of 24 Rafale fighter jets to Qatar at a cost of around £5.7 billion.

*

---

[3]*Ibid.*

In the crowded 'terrorist marketplace' Isis is by far the most toxic brand, with its heinous and murderous acts, the torturing and killing of both innocents and combatants, the public beheadings and burnings, the killings of homosexuals and Christians, the abuse and rape of women, and its wanton destruction of ancient architectural and cultural treasures.

Prior to the advent of Isis it was al-Qaeda that dominated headlines, and at times it was believed that they were one and the same. However, not only is there deep personal animosity between their leaders – 'al-Baghdadi has repeatedly made a point of explicitly repudiating the authority of al-Zawahiri and claiming to be the true inheritor of the legacy of Bin Laden[4] – but, prior to the events of November 2015, they had been seen to possess quite different strategies, with Isis rejecting the 'Far Enemy' strategy in favour of the 'Near Enemy'. As Jason Burke puts it, Isis had shown itself to be most interested in the immediate seizure of territory and local resources, limiting international terror to attacks on tourists in Muslim-majority countries, while also calling for lone actors in Europe and the USA to mount attacks themselves. Most significantly, he notes the fact that the leadership of al-Qaeda has always stressed the need to minimise violence *between Muslims*. By contrast, 'sectarian violence against co-religionists is fundamental to Isis, arguably its raison d'être'.[5] However, with the horrific attacks on Paris and Beirut in November 2015, which left scores of people dead, some have suggested that Isis and its affiliates may have changed their tactics

---

[4]Jason Burke (2015), *The New Threat: From Islamic Militancy*, London: The Bodley Head, p. 17.
[5]*Ibid.*

to include organised assaults on Western targets. This may be a response to growing pressure on their operations in Iraq and Syria. Personally, I strongly condemn these terrible attacks.

Burke also suggests that a number of 'independent' terrorist groups hitherto uninterested in attacking the West may do so in the future. A number of these are to be found in South Asia, an unstable region made more so as the USA continues to withdraw its troops from Afghanistan. In particular, he cites the examples of the Afghan Taliban, the Pakistani Taliban and Lashkar-e-Taiba, the Pakistan-based group responsible for the 2008 attacks in Mumbai.[6]

As I travel through the Middle East, in Jordan, Qatar, Lebanon and elsewhere, talk soon centres on Isis or, as it's known in the region, *Daesh (al-Dawla al-Islamyia fil Iraq wa'al Sham)*. The region's instability is further increased by the involvement, on different and opposing sides, of a number of the more established world powers: Iran, Russia and China on one side, and the USA, Europe and the Gulf States on the other.

Some have suggested that *Daesh*'s finances come predominantly from its Wahhabi supporters. Wahhabism is a division of Sunni Islam, whose rigidity and 'orthodoxy' has led it to misinterpret and distort Islam, leading to extremists such as the Taliban. *Daesh* (also known by its longer name, the Islamic State of Iraq and the Levant) also draws on Wahhabism for its hateful ideology.

The ideology of Wahhabism stems from the eighteenth-century preacher and scholar Muhammad ibn Abd al-Wahhab (1703–92),

[6]*Ibid.*

who started a revivalist movement in the remote, sparsely populated region of Najd, where he advocated the purging of practices such as popular shrine and tomb visitation, widespread among Muslims, but which he considered idolatry. Eventually he formed a pact with a local leader, Muhammad bin Saud, offering political obedience and promising that protection and propagation of the Wahhabi movement would mean 'power and glory'.

The alliance between followers of ibn Abd al-Wahhab and Muhammad bin Saud's successors (the House of Saud) has proved durable. The House of bin Saud continued to maintain its politico-religious alliance with the Wahhabi sect over the following 150 years, through to its eventual proclamation of the Kingdom of Saudi Arabia in 1932, and then afterwards, into modern times. Today Mohammed bin Abd Al-Wahhab's teachings are state-sponsored and are the official form of Sunni Islam in twenty-first-century Saudi Arabia.

Wahhabis are present in Qatar, the United Arab Emirates and Saudi Arabia, and indeed they are the 'dominant minority' in Saudi Arabia, with four million Saudi Wahhabis (concentrated in Najd) representing over 20 per cent of the population. The movement underwent considerable growth at the beginning of the 1970s and now has worldwide influence. Wahhabi mosques and preachers are now located throughout the world, including in Europe and America. Indeed Wahhabism's contemporary growth began in the 1970s, when Saudi charities started funding Wahhabi schools and mosques. Michael Burleigh, a fierce critic of Wahhabism, reminds us that we are repeatedly told of the need to tackle the kind of 'extremism' that breeds so-called 'Islamic terrorism', but adds that:

A good place to start would be Saudi Arabia's global campaign of political-religious subversion through its funding of extremist schools, or madrassas, around the Middle East, north Africa, Pakistan and Afghanistan.[7]

I personally cannot make sense of the contemporary significance of the Sunni–Shia division. When I was living in Kuwait, at the time of the first Gulf War, I never heard talk of it, even when Saddam Hussein was involved in his murderous struggle with Iran. The division, I believe, was created *after* the Gulf War to divide the whole of the Middle East. And now, of course, all of the Middle East is divided, as in Syria and Yemen, and all because of this sectarian division. As Robert Fisk commented, Saudi Arabia has sent fighters from Egypt, Morocco, Jordan – with the exception of Oman – to fight in Yemen, because they believe the Shia were fighting a proxy war.

Of course the split between Sunni and Shia occurred in the past, at the time of the Prophet's grandson, but in the twenty-first century we should be able to unite and point to similarities rather than differences. Once that is achieved, the geographical, territorial, historical, cultural and other such layers that accentuate the split and division can be stripped away.

I don't consider the leadership and followers of *Daesh* and other similar groups as Muslim. I see them as murderers, extremists and 'outsiders' (*khawraj*). They misinterpret and selectively misquote the Qur'an.

*

---

[7]Michael Burleigh, 'Saudi Arabia, not Iran, is our greatest threat', *The Times*, 4 August 2015, p. 22.

Why has the twenty-first century witnessed the emergence of groups such as Isis? Again I return to Robert Fisk, who succinctly makes the point that one of the reasons is the prior behaviour of the West, as in its various and numerous military and political adventures, including George W. Bush and Tony Blair's 2003 invasion of Iraq. As Fisk puts it, 'if you cause trouble in the Middle East it will come back to haunt you. If you bomb Syria or Iraq, you will pay the price. It's inevitable. And, if after that you then go and mock the religion of the people who have died in such numbers, well then some people are going to be very angry.'[8] Isis is obviously not a 'state', but a cult. They are as dangerous, as flamboyant, as horrible and as ridiculous as other cults that have previously existed. Fisk adds:

> It's fairly clear to me that Isis emerged from the brutality, cruelty and sectarianism that followed the Western invasion of Iraq. In the years that followed I would go to a mortuary and see bodies coming in without heads, with slit throats. I remember hearing of one body that had a dog's head sewn on in place of its own – that was the beginning of Isis. *And like all cults it will split.*[9]

It is evident that Isis rose from the ashes of Iraq. As a child and young man I visited Baghdad with my family, especially my dad, and enjoyed happy and interesting times there. Recently when I was in Iraq, it bore no resemblance to the beautiful city I vividly remember. It's hard to imagine that at one time – in fact, for much of the Abbasid era

---

[8] A conversation with Robert Fisk, www.thejournal.ie, 21 March 2015.
[9] *Ibid.*

(762–1258 AD) – Baghdad was 'the most eminent seat of science and learning', the most sophisticated city in the world.[10]

As I did, Fisk saw the events in Paris following the *Charlie Hebdo* murders, where politicians and the public marched through the streets of Paris in 'solidarity', as somewhat confusing: 'We saw a march through Paris led by people with blood on their hands, a Saudi diplomat from a country which chops off heads, an Israeli prime minister whose country had slaughtered children the previous August; what were they marching for?'[11]

*

So what is to be done?

There is no doubt that Isis is evil, a cult that massacres its opponents, slaughters civilians, beheads the innocent, rapes children and enslaves women. At one level it is alarmingly more 'developed' and organised than is imagined – 'ID cards are issued in Isis-land, the river police have newly painted boats, taxes are raised'[12] – but sadly their killings and punishments remain barbarous.

Of course, as an Arab, I am constantly drawn into this miasmic environment of madness, terrorism and death, and I always ask myself the question: 'What are Arab countries – other than Saudi Arabia – doing to try and bring this terror to an end?' In particular, I ask following the recent killings of Palestinians in Gaza in 2014: 'Why didn't the various Arab countries fight for their fellow Muslims?'

---

[10]See John Robertson (2015), *Iraq*, London: Oneworld.
[11]Fisk, 21 March 2015, *op. cit.*
[12]Robert Fisk, *Independent*, 27 July 2015.

Of course, I know the answer to my own question, namely that various geopolitical and petrodollar interests ensure that they do nothing, and that self-interest always comes first. But even among my fellow Arabs, it's evident that many have bought the American version of reality ('terror') and have neglected to investigate the underlying causes of injustice.

Change in Saudi Arabia is taking place, and in my optimistic moments I believe that the movement towards a more moderate stance has begun. It will, however, be extremely difficult to bring about the necessary meaningful change, and there are many obstacles. For example, consider the mere fact that there are over 45,000 princes and princesses in Saudi Arabia, with so much money that they are able to spend vast amounts of time and investment in the West, in the UK, the USA and such places as the South of France.

Like Britain, France sells millions of pounds' worth of arms to Saudi Arabia every year and considers the country one of its greatest allies. Indeed, France has been nurturing new links with Saudi Arabia and other Gulf Arab countries over the past three years, due to its tough stance on Iran and similar positions on conflicts across the Middle East. It is beginning to see commercial rewards in terms of contracts for companies in the energy and defence sectors. And this is why the Ministry of the Interior in Paris is thought to have agreed to keep all women officers away from the Saudis as requested by the king on a recent trip to the South of France.[13] However, unlike the older Saudi citizens who continue to receive their 'news' from Al Jazeera, CNN

---

[13] 'Saudi King cuts short stay in South of France', *Guardian*, 3 August 2015.

and government-approved media, younger Saudis use social media, especially Facebook and Twitter, which provides them with a quite different account of the events in their country and its international ventures.

Throughout the Middle East, a citizen cannot utter a negative word or express an opinion about a leader without risking an encounter with the authorities. In Jordan, my country, I believe that King Abdullah wants to change the way the country operates, despite some of the voices in opposition to him. King Abdullah's wife, Queen Rania Al-Abdullah, works tirelessly for progressive women's and children's charities throughout Jordan, but is constantly criticised because of her views on women's issues and other important problems. I have so much respect for the queen; she is doing amazing work and is a great example for women in the Arab world.

There are issues in Jordan too. Jordan has, in 2015, signed a huge and controversial gas deal with Israel, with the long arm of the USA behind it. I oppose this deal, as does BDS, who have vigorously campaigned against it.

Another iniquity and injustice I recently learned of on a visit to Amman concerned government teachers who, in Jordan, receive so small a salary that they're unable to look after their families in any reasonable way. Apparently, when the IMF (International Monetary Fund) stepped in to help this situation, they insisted that changes be made to the school curriculum, favouring Israel. However, students protested for six months and, as a result, some concessions were eventually made to this distorted curriculum.

*

I learned about *jihad* when I lived in Jordan. In essence I see it as follows: if someone tries to kill my family, or me, tries to take my house and home away from me, I will fight back. That's one version of *jihad*. And if I die when I fight, I go to heaven. But I was always taught that *jihad* did not mean that someone could go to someone else's home, country or land, and attack them. The only *jihad* that the whole of the Muslim world agrees with is the rightful and justifiable Palestinian fight against the Israeli occupation. However, I also learned about the *internal jihad*. This is all about being a 'good Muslim', behaving properly, following *Sharia*. I see the struggles I undertake – climbing mountains and giving speeches and seminars, trying to raise an income for my family – as a *jihad*. I take the BDS flag to the top of the mountain, defending my faith and beliefs, and that's also a *jihad*.

It is essential that the billion-plus Muslims in the world are not judged by the behaviour and example of the 1 per cent of people like *Daesh*, in the same way that I do not judge the Roman Catholic Church by the behaviour of a tiny number of paedophile priests.

I grew up with a Palestinian father, then lived in Amman and was granted a Jordanian passport. Later still, I was granted British citizenship. I see myself as both Palestinian and Jordanian, and also British. I try to teach my children the idea that they should choose whichever religion they favour. Their mother, Krissy, my wife, is a practising and church-attending Christian. At the moment, for bureaucratic reasons, they are British and Christian, but I nevertheless teach them about my religion and take them to the mosque and read the Qur'an to them. In fact, both Krissy and I read to them from both of the holy books. When they're older I'll tell them about the history and tragedy of Palestine.

And another thing they'll learn about are the double standards that are applied when Islam and other religions, especially Christianity, are contrasted and compared.

*

The media distorts, misrepresents and, at times, blatantly engages in *Islamophobia* (dislike or prejudice against Islam and/or Muslims). On an almost daily basis I encounter an obvious and pervasive double standard.

For example, I was outraged at the manner in which the tragic case of the 2011 Norwegian killings was reported. This concerned the Norwegian killer Anders Behring Breivik, invariably described as a 'far-right terrorist'. On 22 July he killed eight people by setting off a van bomb amid government buildings in Oslo, and then shot dead 69 young participants of a Workers' Youth League (AUF) summer camp on the island of Utøya. Hours before the attacks, Breivik emailed a 1,500-page manifesto to 5,700 people, titled *2083 – A European Declaration of Independence*. In this document he attacked multiculturalism and, in particular, the threat that Muslim immigration posed to Norway. He wrote that he was Christianity's saviour and claimed to be a member of the Order of Knights Templar.

At the time, Breivik was also well known as being extremely active on various anti-Muslim websites. Later, under questioning, he claimed that he actually belonged to an unnamed organisation that possessed active and undetected terror cells. On August 2012, Breivik was convicted of three offences: mass murder, causing a fatal explosion, and terrorism.

Now, we all know that Breivik's motive was religious. We aren't stupid enough to believe that his violent and murderous acts were unconnected with his hatred of Islam. So why didn't the media and society at large describe him as a 'Christian extremist'? I could pose the same question about another murderer: why wasn't American-Israeli Baruch Goldstein – a member of the far-right Israeli Kach movement – called a 'Jewish extremist'? This is the man who, on 25 February 1994, opened fire on a large number of Palestinian Muslims who had gathered to pray inside the Ibrahimi Mosque (*Mosque of Abraham*) at the Cave of the Patriarchs in Hebron, West Bank. The attack left 29 dead and 125 wounded, before Goldstein was overpowered and beaten to death by survivors. The massacre itself immediately set off mass Palestinian protests and riots throughout the West Bank, and tragically within 48 hours another nine Palestinian protesters had been killed by the Israeli Defence Forces. Goldstein was widely denounced in Israel, with many attributing his act to insanity.

Compare the media's representation of Breivik with that of the two British Nigerian men, Michael Adebolajo and Michael Adebowale, who savagely killed the British soldier Lee Rigby on the streets of south London. They were invariably and unanimously described as 'Islamic terrorists', not British extremists or murderers or 'insane' individuals.

*

The so-called 'radicalisation' in recent decades of young men and women, who may subsequently act 'in the name of Islam', occurs in part because of such double standards. And of course, as I've said, the illegal war carried out by George W. Bush and Tony Blair and their allies, in Iraq, is another factor. The anger at Blair's involvement in this tragic and bloody adventure was exacerbated when he was later inconceivably appointed as a 'peace' envoy in the Middle East for the so-called Quartet (the US, EU, UN and Russia), and more recently when he was appointed to head the European Council on Tolerance and Reconciliation (ECTR), Europe's major Zionist lobby group (which, some say, systematically shields Zionist and Israeli crimes).

I take a great interest in this so-called radicalisation, and spend much of my time working with young people in the Arab world who are perceived as being vulnerable to it.

In an informative article, Shiraz Maher asks the question, 'What links a white Englishman from Buckinghamshire with a second-generation British-Asian man born in Dewsbury and a missing family of 12 from Bradford?'[14] The answer, of course, is that all are believed to have left the UK in 2015 to support various *jihadist* causes overseas.

As Maher argues, cases like these demonstrate that 'radicalisation' involves many factors, and that this is frequently lost in polarised public debates that either identify variable readings of the Qur'an as the sole reason for all terrorism or, conversely, blame everything on government policies, past or present. Rather, he continues, if all the grievances and myriad individual triggers that might drive an individual to join an extremist group are stripped away, what remain are the underlying issues of identity and belonging.[15]

---

[14]Shiraz Maher, 'The roots of radicalisation? It's identity, stupid', *ICSR Insight*, 23 June 2015.
[15]*Ibid.*

This is not new. For instance, when Mohammad Sidique Khan led the 7/7 London terrorist attacks a decade ago, he claimed that his actions were in retaliation for 'the bombing, gassing, imprisonment and torture of my people'. Maher poses another question regarding Khan, asking, 'Isn't it the case that Khan was killing his own people, the ordinary citizen-stranger commuting to work, when he detonated his bomb on the London Underground?' while claiming he was identifying with Iraqis, from a country he'd never travelled to and whose language he couldn't speak?[16]

*

In my opinion, the simple quick-fix solution of somehow trying to inculcate so-called 'British values' in British Muslims is unlikely to be successful. Times have changed since the period when Britain was able to mobilise the largest volunteer army in history to fight fascism, when hundreds of thousands of Muslims from across the empire fought for the British cause during the First and Second World Wars.

Some Muslim leaders are critical of this 'values' approach. They regard any discussion of British values as a hostile attempt to engineer a new and diluted form of Islam. Maher suggests that governments will have to scale back the 'values' approach and, instead, accept that some Muslims *wish* to live highly orthodox and segregated lives, which is their right in an open and democratic society. But, he adds, if such Muslims resist this governmental approach, then they must 'propose

---

[16]*Ibid.*

an alternative model to resolve the underlying issues of identity and belonging that play a significant role in the radicalisation of so many', as it cannot 'be enough for the West to accommodate Islam – Islam must also accommodate the West'.[17]

Neither is it helpful to presume that all the 'undesirable' political beliefs and behaviour of young Muslims are a result of 'brainwashing' of some sort or another, nor to presume that such young people are necessarily vulnerable and naïve. The young are commonly deemed to be easy prey for those seeking to enlist them for a so-called 'radical' cause. Indeed, children and young people's engagement in 'oppositional politics' has often been explained away by reference to their supposed psychological immaturity. Outside of state-sanctioned exceptions (such as allowing 16- and 17-year-olds to vote in the Scottish referendum), political engagement by minors is liable to be dismissed as the product of mental or physical coercion, the incapacity associated with immaturity, or a combination of both.[18]

This unwillingness to seriously consider why children and young people might engage in armed hostilities is relatively new, and is liable to occur when those concerned fight for causes we consider objectionable. Jason Hart contrasts the situation of a century ago, when 'the estimated 250,000 boys who volunteered to fight for the British Army were hailed by newspaper editors and political leaders as heroes and patriots, not dupes or truants'.[19]

---

[17]*Ibid.*

[18]Jason Hart, 'Brainwashing and radicalisation don't explain why young people join violent causes', www.theconversation.com/uk, 1 December 2014.

[19]*Ibid.*

Various European governments have been alarmed when their young citizens have turned to 'extremist' groups or committed terrible acts in their name, but few have stopped to think about how their own policies have contributed to the problem. Hart makes an important and careful observation:

> For decades, European countries have made it difficult for young people to be pious Muslims and feel European at the same time. But that hasn't stopped them, it has simply taught them that their new-found faith may not be compatible with their European life. That in turn makes them all the more vulnerable.[20]

Islam is now a significant part of the youthful, racially and ethnically mixed urban culture that exists in Europe and North America. In addition, thousands of Europeans convert to Islam and many ethnic Muslims who did not grow up in religious homes are introduced to Islam through friends and colleagues. Converted or born-again newcomers to Islam who find religion on their own often don't fully understand that there are many different interpretations of Islam.[21] Instead, they try to learn about their faith either on the Internet or through local mosques, and, of course, many attend puritan Salafi mosques, which promote the idea of leaving all Western traditions behind to try and emulate the life of the Prophet Muhammad.

The Salafi movement is an ultra-conservative sect within Sunni Islam and is often divided into three categories: the largest group, the purists (or quietists), who avoid politics; the second-largest group,

---

[20]*Ibid.*
[21]*Ibid.*

the activists, who get involved in politics; and the smallest group, the *jihadists*, who form a tiny and infamous minority. Salafism has become associated with literalist, strict and puritanical approaches to Islam and, particularly in the West, with the Salafi *jihadists*.

Salafists in Europe proselytise more than adherents of any other branch of Islam, but, as Jason Hart points out, the majority of Salafi communities across Europe 'are not jihadist, and even stay away from political engagement. Most converts or born-again Muslims, especially those with a criminal past, find their lives are significantly *improved* by joining Salafi communities'.[22] The problem emerges when Salafi *jihadists* recruit young and impressionable new Muslims and cut them off from non-Muslims, or other branches of Islam, and also encourage them to turn their backs on their families and friends.

European Muslim converts are an excellent resource for *jihadists*, as they come with money, mobility, linguistic ability and technological 'knowhow'.

For decades, many European governments have made life difficult for European Muslims, supporting mosques that centre on one or another distinct national group rather than making it possible for people to receive Islamic education in their local language. Consequently, various governments have enabled Imams who do not speak the local language and know nothing of local culture or issues to dominate the preaching and teaching. These policies have ensured that most mosques do not speak to the realities of young people in their areas. Salafi mosques are 'streets ahead of national mosques in tuning into European culture

---

[22]*Ibid.*

and life and are an appealing option as a result'.[23] Hart's conclusions are practical and, from my experience of the UK, especially in Luton and London, both urgent and necessary:

> The solution to the integration of Muslims is also an answer to radicalisation. European governments should trust and support individuals and organisations that promote being both Europeans and pious Muslims. They should encourage Islamic education in the local language and stop treating converts as threats to the nation. Being European and a pious Muslim should not feel like a devious act that can be practised only away from mainstream society...[as that]...will make it easier for *jihadists* to appeal to young Muslim converts and born-again Muslims.[24]

British Muslim Syed Kamall says he underwent a considerable amount of soul-searching following the *Charlie Hebdo* attack, and asked himself the question, how have we 'arrived at the point where young Muslim men would rather kill their neighbours in the name of "Allah" than live normal, peaceful lives?'[25] In a similar vein to Jason Hart, he states that there is no contradiction between being Muslim and being British or European. As he asserts, his religion is as much a part of his identity as being British or a proud Londoner: 'Faith aside, I probably have more in common with a Christian in Peckham than with a Muslim in Peshawar', and to 'me and other British Muslims like me, our identity is clear. But for many younger people an identity crisis isn't uncommon, regardless of their

---

[23]*Ibid.*

[24]*Ibid.*

[25]Syed Kamall, *Wall Street Journal*, 5 February 2015.

religion. Some teenagers react by rebelling. Others, more extreme, will turn to crime and gangs'.[26]

In the simplest sense, it can be reasonably argued that Islam teaches that our lives are a struggle, or a *jihad*, a struggle to live a good life and refrain from bad deeds. At the end of our lives, we will be judged on whether the good deeds outweigh the bad. Those who seek to radicalise argue that the good Muslim life cannot be lived in decadent modern Western societies. The so-called 'radicalisers' anger the young by showing them propaganda and images of Muslims being killed by Western forces in Middle Eastern conflicts, and, as a result, convince them that there is a shortcut to paradise through revenge in the name of Allah. An angry young person undergoing an identity crisis might well believe such misguided misinformation. Kamall's suggestions as to how to combat 'radicalisation' include the important role of the imam:

> Our religious leaders must also be vigilant. The imam at my local mosque recently preached that if a cartoon offends us, our response should be to say 'peace'. However, I have visited mosques in Europe where sermons aren't preached in the local language, potentially excluding younger people or giving them only a partial understanding of what is being taught. Left confused and frustrated, they become prime targets for radical recruiters outside the mosque offering literature in the local language. Invited to meetings in the local language, they may be radicalised by being taught a wholly selective version of Islam.[27]

---

[26]*Ibid.*
[27]*Ibid.*

*

As a parent myself, married to a woman who is a Christian, I believe it is important to help a child's ever-growing sense of identity by encouraging them to mix with people from all backgrounds. This *may* help to prevent a child, yours or mine, becoming the victim of radicalisation.

The Internet is a powerful force, especially on the minds of individuals who are naive. Therefore, we must pay attention to the personality and behaviour of the parents of young Muslims – which mosques do they attend, which preachers do they listen to, what do they tell their children about both Islam and also other religions, and how much time do they spend with them, asking and answering questions?

The influence of the Internet cannot be underestimated. My own professional life depends on it: within seconds of touching a keyboard, I raise money and make sustained and productive relationships. Robert Fisk has argued that Isis has turned the Internet into the most effective propaganda tool ever. In fact, he wonders whether Isis 'isn't more real on the Internet than it is on the ground' – not, of course, for the Kurds of Kobani or the Yazidis or the beheaded victims of 'this weird caliphate' – but, nevertheless, he adds, 'Isn't it time we woke up to the fact that Internet addiction in politics and war is even more dangerous than hard drugs?'[28] In other words, it is not Isis that radicalises the youthful, vulnerable or isolated, but the Internet. As Fisk puts it:

---

[28]Robert Fisk, 'On Isis: Propaganda war of Islamic extremists is being waged on Facebook and Internet message boards, not mosques', *Independent*, 12 October 2014.

In Lebanon, for example, there is some evidence that pictures on YouTube have just as much influence upon Muslims who suddenly decide to travel to Syria and Iraq as do Sunni preachers. Photographs of Sunni Muslim victims – or of the 'execution' of their supposedly apostate enemies – have a powerful impact out of all proportion to words on their own.[29]

An Agence France-Presse report in 2014 told of a 15-year-old girl from Avignon who left for the Syrian war without telling her parents. Her brother discovered she led parallel lives, with two Facebook accounts, one where she talked about her normal teenage life, another where she wrote about her desire to go 'to Aleppo to help our Syrian brothers and sisters'. Research suggests that 'radicalisation' through the Internet can take place over a short duration, sometimes as short as a month. It reminds Fisk of the 'accounts of American teenagers who lock themselves on to the Internet for hours before storming off to shoot their school colleagues and teachers'.[30]

*

When I was recently at a conference in Amman, in which the radicalisation of Jordanian youth was discussed, and the role of the Internet debated and discussed, it didn't take long for the central issue in the Middle Eastern tragedy to be raised. Namely Palestine.

This conflict, this injustice, is at the centre of my work, my politics and my life. Israel has occupied my land. The Israelis constantly talk about the Holocaust and frequently make films about it. But every day

---

[29] *Ibid.*
[30] *Ibid.*

in Gaza and the West Bank there are Holocausts. I passionately want
the BDS to bring Israel to its knees. Perhaps it is already working,
because the Israelis are spending huge amounts of money to stop its
growing influence. BDS is peaceful. What I do, for example, is drink
Pepsi and not Coca-Cola. And I don't shop at Marks and Spencer,
because they send a small percentage of their profits to Israel.

Let the Israelis act with violence, not us.

There has to be hope that all and any Palestinians will one day be
able to return home. My 67-year-old dad would return to Palestine
tomorrow. As he recently said to me, 'I would crawl to Jerusalem on
my knees.'

In his short but concise account of the current state of Palestinian
politics, Raja Shehadeh points to the centrality of the issue and its
implications for the current tragedies. As he puts it:

> The Islamic State of Iraq and the Levant (ISIL) seems to thrive
> on the frustration of people facing seemingly insurmountable
> obstacles in their fight for greater rights and freedom within their
> own states and the failure of the Palestinians to win the liberation
> of their land occupied by Israel over four decades earlier through
> the reliance on peaceful resistance and invocation of the rule of
> law.[31]

In a different context, he also discusses the role of the Internet,
and argues that Isis has learned 'dangerous and brutal lessons from
the repeated failure of Arab states and armies in their fight against
Israel and the Western powers', most notably 'how to manipulate

---

[31]Shehadeh (2014), p. 246.

the media perhaps from Israel's noted success, how to be cured of illusions about the democracy of the West from the actions of the West itself'.[32]

I cannot believe that I've lived my whole life so far, and still Palestine remains occupied and over six million Palestinian refugees exist in alien lands, robbed of their homes.

The issue of Palestine is absolutely central to the turmoil in the Middle East, and has global repercussions. It's obvious that Israel can do whatever it wishes in Palestine and to Palestinian people, because it knows it will always have the support of the USA and particular European nations. With the recent bombings and killings in 2014 of innocent people in Gaza, I waited in vain for censure or even some sort of action from the West. But, of course, it never came. This is why there is so much negativity towards, and, at times, hatred of, the West from supporters of Palestine.

My own view is that fighting or violence or military action will not solve the tragedy. A first step would be for people in the West to be taught precisely what is happening in the occupied lands and to the lives of Palestinian refugees around the world. I'm not the kind of guy who could take up arms on any occasion, or for any cause. For example, when I was in India I often saw Israeli guys smoking dope, and generally hanging out in various cafés, but I never ever thought, 'If only I could somehow get myself a gun, I could take them all out.' It just isn't my way.

Even in Jordan, my dad has always lived as a Palestinian. He still has some land there, which he's never ever thought of selling. Conversely, my dad has never tried to buy land or a house in Jordan, because in his heart and head he always believes that one day he'll return.

I have a British passport, as well as a Jordanian one, but I still cannot visit Palestine because of my involvement with BDS. The Israeli government has unofficially deemed me *persona non grata* and has refused me entry.

In 2013 I was scheduled – and arranged, many months in advance – to deliver a lecture at the Al Najah University, Nablus, and accordingly late one morning I went to the Sheikh Hussein Crossing Bridge. I was due to lecture about my life as a refugee, hotelier and climber, and also about my thoughts on Palestine.

At the Crossing, I presented my British passport. I didn't anticipate any problems. However, for the next ten hours a young Israeli soldier – aged perhaps 19 or 20 – questioned and, at times, intensely and aggressively interrogated me. He appeared not to believe anything I told him and constantly sought to trip me up. He also took my phone from me and passed it to a colleague who looked at my contacts. He then aggressively asked, 'Why do you have a Lebanese number on your phone?' Actually, it was the number of the cocaine dealer I had used in the past whenever I wanted to 'party' in Beirut. But I wasn't going to tell him that. Then the colleague showed me the number of an Iranian contact. I explained that it was the secretary of the Iranian Mountaineering Association, who I'd met on the slopes of Everest. And then, in answer to a direct question, I told them that 'yes, my parents have Palestinian connections – my dad is from Ramallah and my mum from Jaffa'.

After another hour of this unpleasantness, a different soldier appeared, a young woman, who simply said: 'You're not welcome in the State of Israel.' I was annoyed and disappointed, but managed to conceal this and said to her, 'I wasn't coming to Israel, I was coming to Palestine.' They smiled sarcastically. I was desperately upset as I so wanted to see Jerusalem.

Palestine is, for me, not a Muslim problem, not an Arab problem, but rather a problem about freedom: the right of people to return to their homeland. I demand that the United Nations Resolution of 1967 be implemented. The occupation is an international scandal. In the past I always blamed the West for their lack of support for the Palestinians, but social media shines a light on the real scandal: the amount of money in the Gulf and the reluctance of these nations to intervene. These Gulf nations could say to the USA, 'We're going to cut off the oil and gas pipelines to you, unless you intervene in Palestine.' But, then again, the prospect of the USA and her allies acting against Israel is completely remote.

The Middle East is now fragmented. There is no unity. Travelling from one Arab country to another is easier if you are the holder of an American or European passport than an Arabic one. Even if, for example, I visit Dubai on a Jordanian passport, the visa application takes a long time compared with the rapid speed when I travel with my British passport.

So these days I blame the Arabs, not the West. We Arabs and Muslims need to unite: consider the mathematics and ammunition – 1.7 billion Muslims, as opposed to 6 million Israelis. I've met Jews in London, Kashmir and Dublin who said they would never visit Israel, because of the occupation. I respect them. I always try and teach that it's wrong to compare Jews with the Zionists of Israel.

2005 saw the small but significant beginnings of BDS. It was agreed that there was a need for a broad and sustained campaign for 'Boycott, Divestment and Sanctions', and this was launched in July of that year, with the initial endorsement of over 170 Palestinian organisations. The signatories represented the three major components of the Palestinian people: the refugees in exile, Palestinians under occupation in the West Bank and Gaza Strip, and the discriminated Palestinian citizens of the Israeli state. The first Palestinian BDS Conference was held in Ramallah in November 2007, and from this conference emerged the BDS National Committee (BNC), acting as the Palestinian coordinating body for the BDS campaign worldwide.

When Mary Nazzal-Batayneh mentioned the BDS movement to me, I got it immediately. I completely respect her and her judgement. She works tirelessly for the Palestinian cause. Because of BDS I now look at every single product or item I consider buying. I used to enjoy avocados from Israel, which tasted divine, but now I wouldn't dream of buying them. On any climb or expedition or hike that I undertake, I always make sure that I take the BDS flag with me.

The only thing that will genuinely hurt and damage Israel is an attack on their economy. The support for BDS is increasing: note the recent condemnation of Robbie Williams' concerts in Israel by Roger Waters of Pink Floyd, and the publicity it created.

*

It's instructive to consider a brief history of the conflict. Without wishing to repeat what I've already described and what has provided the inspiration for my 2017 climb on Ben Nevis, the conflict has its recent roots in the division of the former British Mandate of Palestine and the creation of the State of Israel in the years after the end of the Second World War – the culmination of the Zionist movement, whose aim was a homeland for Jews hitherto scattered all over the world. After the Nazi Holocaust, pressure grew for the international recognition of a Jewish state, and in 1948 Israel declared its independence following a UN vote to partition Palestine. Much of the history of the region since that time has been one of conflict between Israel on one side and Palestinians – represented by the Palestine Liberation Organization, Hamas and Fatah – and Israel's Arab neighbours on the other. Hundreds of thousands of Palestinian Arabs were displaced in the fighting in 1948, during which Israel's Arab neighbours came to the aid of the Arab Higher Committee in Palestine. Israel lost 1 per cent of its population in the fighting, which ultimately ended in a series of uneasy armistices.

An author and commentator I regularly rely on, and refer to, is American scholar and activist Noam Chomsky, who has courageously spoken out about Palestine for many years. In an interview on the Palestinian struggle to end the occupation he states that the Israel–Palestine conflict appears so 'intractable that it's hard to think of a solution', yet in fact it isn't. On the contrary, he asserts, 'the general outlines of a diplomatic solution have been clear for at least 40 years'.[33]

The basic outlines were presented in New York at the UN Security Council in January 1976. It called for a two-state settlement on

---

[33]'Interview with Noam Chomsky', *Democracy Now!*, 22 October, 2014.

the internationally recognised border and, as Chomsky observes, included the guarantee 'for the rights of both states to exist in peace and security within secure and recognised borders.'[34] The resolution was brought by the three major Arab states, Egypt, Jordan and Syria, but perhaps unsurprisingly Israel refused to attend the session, and in addition the United States exercised its veto. A US veto is typically a 'double veto': in other words, the resolution is not implemented, and then the event is vetoed from history. As Chomsky observes, that set a pattern that has continued ever since.[35]

Indeed, ever since 1976, Israel, with the decisive support of the United States – military, economic, diplomatic and ideological – has devoted extensive resources to ensuring that it will *never* be implemented, by establishing how the conflict is viewed and interpreted throughout the world.

Back to some history.

*

Palestinians in the West Bank and eastern Jerusalem have lived under Israeli occupation since 1967. Israel has developed from an agrarian state run along collectivist lines into a hi-tech economy over the past 60 years, has absorbed Jewish immigrants from Europe, the rest of the Middle East, North America and, most recently, from the former Soviet Union and Ethiopia. Its political life has been dominated by the conflict with its Arab neighbours, including full-scale regional wars in 1948, 1967 and 1973, and many smaller-scale conflicts, including

---

[34]*Ibid.*
[35]*Ibid.*

the 1956 invasion of Egypt and wars with Lebanon in 1982 and 2006. The settlements that Israel has built in the West Bank are home to nearly half a million people and under international law are illegal. The 1967 'Six-Day War' exerted a significant effect upon Palestinian nationalism, as Israel gained authority over the West Bank from Jordan and the Gaza Strip from Egypt. Consequently, the PLO was unable to establish any control on the ground and set up its headquarters in Jordan, home to hundreds of thousands of Palestinians. However, the Palestinian base in Jordan collapsed with the Jordanian–Palestinian civil war in 1970, and the PLO defeat by the Jordanians caused most of the Palestinian militants to relocate to South Lebanon, where they soon took over large areas, creating the so-called 'Fatahland'.

In 1979, Egypt and Israel signed a peace agreement, but it wasn't until the early 1990s, after years of the intifada (uprising), that a peace process began with the Palestinians. Despite the handover of Gaza and parts of the West Bank to Palestinian control, a final agreement was never reached. The main stumbling blocks then, as now, were the status of Jerusalem, the fate of Palestinian refugees and their descendants, and Jewish settlements.

Control of Jerusalem is a particularly delicate issue, with each side claiming this holy city. The three largest Abrahamic religions – Judaism, Christianity and Islam – all hold Jerusalem as an important setting for their religious and historical narratives. For Judaism, it is the former location of the Jewish temples on the Temple Mount and the capital of the ancient Israelite kingdom; for Muslims, Jerusalem is the site of Mohammad's Night Journey to heaven and the al-Aqsa Mosque; and for Christians, the city is the site of Jesus's crucifixion and the Church of the Holy Sepulchre.

However, in 1980, Israel provocatively issued a new law stating that Jerusalem, 'complete and united', is the capital of Israel. No country in the world except Israel has recognised this.

The first Palestinian intifada began in 1987 as a response to the occupation. By the early 1990s, international efforts to settle the conflict had begun, and eventually the Israeli–Palestinian peace process led to the Oslo Accords of 1993, allowing the PLO to relocate from Tunisia and take ground in the West Bank and Gaza Strip, thus establishing the Palestinian National Authority. The peace process also had significant opposition among radical Islamic elements, such as Hamas and Palestinian Islamic Jihad, who immediately initiated a campaign of attacks targeting Israelis. In 1996, following hundreds of casualties and a wave of radical anti-government propaganda, an Israeli fanatic who objected to the policy of the government assassinated Israeli Prime Minister Rabin. This struck a serious blow to the peace process, from which the newly elected government of Israel backed off.

Following several years of unsuccessful negotiations, the conflict re-erupted as the second intifada in September 2000. In July 2003, the Israeli government initiated the construction of a security barrier following scores of suicide bombings and terrorist attacks, which Israel's coalition government approved in the northern part of the green line between Israel and the West Bank. The violence, escalating into an open conflict between the Palestinian Authority security forces and the Israel Defence Forces (IDF), lasted until 2004/2005 and led Israeli Prime Minister Sharon to disengage from Gaza. In 2005 Israel removed every soldier and every Jewish settler from Gaza. Israel and its Supreme Court formally declared an end to occupation.

In January 2006, a very important event took place: the first full, free election in the Arab world, carefully monitored and recognised to be free and fair. But, as Chomsky points out, 'It had one flaw. It came out the wrong way: Hamas won control of the Parliament. The US and Israel didn't want that.'[36] The US instantly decided, along with Israel, to punish the Palestinians for the crime of voting the wrong way: a harsh siege was instigated, violence increased, and the United States immediately began to organise a military coup to overthrow the 'unacceptable government'. The European Union, to its shame, went along with this. Israel responded that it would begin economic sanctions unless Hamas agreed to accept prior Israeli–Palestinian agreements, forswear violence and recognise Israel's right to exist. And, in 2007, Israel imposed a naval blockade on the Gaza Strip, and in cooperation with Egypt allowed a ground blockade of the Egyptian border.

To briefly fast-forward to April 2014, the Palestinians were then considered by Israel to have committed yet another crime: Gaza-based Hamas and the West Bank-based Palestinian Authority signed an agreement of unity. Israel was angered, especially as most of the world supported this agreement. A unity government undermined one of the pretexts for Israel's refusal to participate in negotiations seriously – namely their previous assertion that negotiations could not take place with an entity that is internally divided. Israel was infuriated. As a consequence, it launched major assaults on the Palestinians in the West Bank, primarily targeting Hamas.

*

---

[36]*Ibid.*

Many attempts have been made to broker a two-state solution, involving the creation of an independent Palestinian state alongside the State of Israel. According to many varied polls the majority of both Israelis and Palestinians prefer the two-state solution to any other. Moreover, a majority of Jews see the Palestinians' demand for an independent state as just, and think Israel can agree to the establishment of such a state.[37] Nonetheless, mutual distrust and significant disagreements remain over basic issues, as does reciprocal scepticism about the other side's commitment to upholding obligations in any eventual agreement.

A hallmark of the conflict has been the level of violence witnessed for virtually its entire duration, wherein fighting has been conducted by regular armies, paramilitary groups, terror cells and murderous individuals. Casualties have not been restricted to the military, with thousands of innocent civilians – children, women, the elderly – also being targeted, maimed and killed.

In a report published in February 2014 covering incidents over the three-year period of 2011–2013, Amnesty International asserted that Israeli forces employed reckless violence in the West Bank, and in some instances appeared to engage in wilful killings which would be tantamount to war crimes.[38] Besides the numerous fatalities, Amnesty said at least 261 Palestinians, including 67 children, had been gravely injured by the Israeli use of live ammunition. In this same period, 45 Palestinians, including 6 children, had been killed. Amnesty's review of 25 civilians' deaths concluded that in no case was there evidence

---

[37]See, for example, Melanie Lidman, 'Support growing for two-state solution', *Jerusalem Post*, 28 December 2011.

[38]Amnesty International, February 2014.

of the Palestinians posing an imminent threat. At the same time, over 8,000 Palestinians suffered serious injuries from other means, including rubber-coated metal bullets. Only one Israeli Defence Forces soldier was convicted, when he killed a Palestinian attempting to enter Israel illegally; he was demoted and given a one-year sentence with a five-month suspension.

*

It is clear to me, as it would be to any reasonable observer, that within both the Israeli and the Palestinian sides of the conflict there exist moderate and extremist bodies, doves as well as hawks. In the absence of extensive representative research on the matter it could surely be assumed that the majority of families on both sides of the conflict wish for peace for their families and themselves.

But the central injustice of the occupation remains.

*

The number of Palestinians who fled or were expelled from Israel following its creation was estimated, in 1949, at something like 711,000. Descendants of these original Palestinian refugees are also eligible for both registration and available services provided by the United Nations Relief and Works Agency for Palestine Refugees in the Near East (UNRWA), and in 2010 they numbered 4.7 million. Additionally, between 350,000 and 400,000 Palestinians were displaced during the 1967 Arab–Israeli war. A third of the refugees live in recognised refugee camps in Jordan, Lebanon, Syria, the West Bank and Gaza Strip, and the remainder live in and around the cities and towns of these host countries.

Most of these refugees were born outside of Palestine, but are descendants of original Palestinian refugees. Palestinian negotiators – from Yasser Arafat onwards – have publicly insisted that refugees have a right to return to the villages, towns and cities where they lived before 1948 and 1967, citing the Universal Declaration of Human Rights and UN General Assembly Resolution 194. However, according to reports of *private* peace negotiations, negotiators have countenanced the return of only 10,000 refugees and their families to Israel as part of a peace settlement. In a private discussion, Mahmoud Abbas, President of the State of Palestine, was once reported to have said that it was absolutely 'illogical to ask Israel to take five million, or indeed one million…[as]…that would mean the end of Israel'.[39]

Compare the situation of the Palestinian refugees with that of the Jews: the Israeli 'Law of Return' that grants citizenship to any Jew from anywhere in the world is a clear form of discrimination against non-Jews, especially the Palestinians who cannot apply for such citizenship or return to the territory from which they were expelled.

It's worth noting that, according to the UN Resolution 194, adopted in 1948, 'the refugees wishing to return to their homes and live at peace with their neighbours should be permitted to do so at the earliest practicable date, and that compensation should be paid for the property of those choosing not to return and for loss of or damage to property which, under principles of international law or in equity, should be made good by the Governments or authorities

---

[39]Ian Black and Seumas Milne, 'Papers reveal how Palestinian leaders gave up fight over refugees', *Guardian*, 24 January 2011.

responsible'. And UN Resolution 3236, approved on 22 November 1974, 'reaffirms also the inalienable right of the Palestinians to return to their homes and property from which they have been displaced and uprooted, and calls for their return'.

The Israeli government asserts that the Arab 'refugee problem' is largely caused by the refusal of all Arab governments, with the exception of Jordan, to grant citizenship to Palestinian Arabs who reside within those countries' borders. The Israelis argue that this has produced much of the poverty and economic problems of the refugees. This is missing the point: *the Palestinians are refugees because of the occupation!*

Israeli forces have launched attacks against Palestinians around the globe as part of the conflict and have assassinated dozens of Palestinians and their supporters outside of Palestine, mainly in Europe and the Middle East. Israel has also bombed Palestinian targets in many nations such as Syria and Lebanon, including the bombing of the PLO Headquarters in Tunisia, killing several hundred.

A report was released by the UN in August 2012 and Maxwell Gaylard, the UN Resident and Humanitarian Coordinator in the occupied Palestinian territory, explained at the launch of the publication that 'Gaza will have half a million more people by 2020 while its economy will grow only slowly' and, as a consequence, 'the people of Gaza will have an even harder time getting enough drinking water and electricity, or sending their children to school'.[40] The report projects that Gaza's population will increase from 1.6 million to 2.1 million people in 2020, leading to a density of more than

---

[40]UN, August 2012.

5,800 people per square kilometre. Compare this with, say, Qatar (175 per square kilometre), Cyprus (146) and Thailand (131).

'Occupied Palestinian Territory' is the term used by the United Nations to refer to the West Bank, including East Jerusalem, and the Gaza Strip – territories that were captured by Israel during the 1967 Six-Day War, having formerly been controlled by Egypt and Jordan. The Israeli government uses the term 'Disputed Territories' to argue that some territories cannot be called 'occupied', as no nation had clear rights to them and there was no operative diplomatic arrangement when Israel acquired them in June 1967. The area is still referred to as Judea and Samaria by some Israeli groups, based on names from ancient times.

According to Oxfam, because of an import-export ban imposed on Gaza in 2007, 95 per cent of its industrial operations were suspended. Out of 35,000 people employed by 3,900 factories in June 2005, only 1,750 people remained employed by 195 factories in June 2007. By 2010, Gaza's unemployment rate had risen to 40 per cent, with 80 per cent of the population living on less than two dollars a day. According to the United Nations Office for the Coordination of Humanitarian Affairs, the Israeli government's continued land, sea and air blockade is tantamount to collective punishment of the population.[41]

In January 2008, the Israeli government calculated how many calories per person were needed to prevent a humanitarian crisis in the Gaza Strip, and then subtracted 8 per cent to adjust for what they termed the 'culture and experience' of the Gazans.

---

[41]The United Nations Office for the Coordination of Humanitarian Affairs, *The Humanitarian Monitor*, December Overview, 2011, OCHA, 31 December 2011.

Moreover, in the past, Israel has demanded control over border crossings between the Palestinian territories and Jordan and Egypt, and the right to set import and export controls, asserting that Israel and the Palestinian territories are a single economic space. With the construction of the West Bank separation barrier, the Israeli state promised free movement across regions. However, border closures, curfews and checkpoints have significantly restricted Palestinian movement. The number of fixed checkpoints reached 99 by 2012, with an additional 310 'flying checkpoints'. The border restrictions impacted imports and exports in Palestine, and weakened the industrial and agricultural sectors because of constant Israeli control in the West Bank and Gaza.

*

The Israelis have never wished the Palestinians to build up an army capable of offensive operations, considering that the only party against which such an army could be turned in the near future is Israel itself. However, Palestinians, quite understandably, have argued that the Israel Defence Forces, a large and modern force, pose a direct and pressing threat to the sovereignty of any future Palestinian state, making a defensive force for a Palestinian state a matter of necessity.

*

In January and February 2015 I participated in a film documentary with director Robert Mullan and his colleagues, which focused on my story and also my perception of the Palestinian tragedy, especially in terms of the way that the majority of refugees live in Jordan and Lebanon. While making the film I met many fascinating people – the elderly, children, the articulate, the passionate – and one who impressed me greatly was Norwegian surgeon and Palestinian activist Dr Mads Gilbert. We filmed part of a lecture he gave at the Landmark Hotel in Amman, at the behest of BDS Jordan, and I was also privileged enough to interview him.

In his harrowing audiovisual lecture, Gilbert described his work in Gaza over a number of years, especially in the summer of 2014 at the al-Shifa Hospital in Gaza City. Gilbert's book, based on his work at al-Shifa, begins with a foreword by Jewish journalist Max Blumenthal:

> …waves of survivors poured from Shuja'iyya into Gaza City… Sons had carried their fathers on their backs; mothers had hoisted children into lorries and ambulances; others searched frantically for missing family when they arrived, only to learn that they had fallen under the shelling. For many, it was another *Nakba*, a hellish reincarnation of the fateful days of 1948 when Zionist militias forcibly expelled hundreds of thousands of Palestinians from their land.[42]

Blumenthal adds that, by dawn, a parade of ambulances was lined up at the gates of Gaza City's al-Shifa Hospital, unloading the wounded 'whose limbs had been chewed up by the hailstorm of Israeli shrapnel'.

Gilbert started working in the region much earlier, when he arrived on emergency assignment for the Norwegian Aid Committee (NORWAC) with the surgeon Erik Fosse, to support the humanitarian effort at the al-Shifa Hospital during the 2008–2009 Israel–Gaza

---

[42]'The Home of the Brave', Foreword by Max Blumenthal, in Mads Gilbert (2015), *Night in Gaza*, Newbold-on-Stour: Skyscraper Publications, pp. 10–13.

conflict, a period when foreign journalists were barred from entering the Gaza Strip. Gilbert, however, maintained frequent contact with Norwegian media, as well as segments of the world press, including CNN, BBC, ABC and Al Jazeera.

Following a grenade strike on a Gaza City vegetable market, on 3 January 2009, Gilbert sent an urgent text message to his Norwegian and international contacts, with an appeal for all who read it to pass it on:

> People in Gaza must know that they are not on their own, many people are with them, although we are not there but we are with them and they must not give up, for the people of the free world ponder on your patience and inspire from your strength. If you give up then the people behind you will give up.

On 5 January, after 10 days of the Israeli heavy air bombardment on the Gaza Strip, Gilbert described the situation inside the al-Shifa Hospital, and said that an overwhelming majority of the casualties he had treated were civilians, and that women and children alone made up 25 per cent of the death toll, as well as 45 per cent of the wounded. This targeting of women and children by the Israeli military was something that Gilbert repeated in his Landmark lecture. He reiterated the point that, whereas Palestinian fighters targeted Israeli combatants, the Israeli military targeted the innocents, especially women and children.

Gilbert and Fosse were subsequently received as heroes by the Norwegian public, and received praise from commentators from most of the mainstream political spectrum for their work during the Gaza War. Labour Party Foreign Minister Jonas Gahr Støre and former Conservative Prime Minister Kåre Willoch both wrote endorsements for Gilbert and Fosse's 2009 book, *Eyes in Gaza*, and Kåre Willoch wrote that 'Israel held journalists away while subjecting the people of Gaza to unfathomable suffering', but two 'Norwegian doctors were there. Their powerful narration throws a powerful spotlight on a brutality which also damages Israel, and impedes peace'.[43]

In an open letter to the medical journal the *Lancet*, Gilbert and Fosse described the Gaza situation as a 'nightmarish havoc', stating that they had 'witnessed the most horrific war injuries in men, women and children of all ages in numbers almost too large to comprehend'. Later, the *Lancet* editor-in-chief, Professor Richard Horton, published a retraction and apologised for publishing the letter.

Gilbert sees things differently, and at the Landmark lecture he argued that medicine and politics were inseparable; he said that the two roles are indistinguishable, and that 'there is *little* in medicine that isn't politics'. Further, he encouraged people to boycott Médecins Sans Frontières, for example, for not taking a position on conflicts. He also campaigned against the training of Norwegian medical personnel assigned to the ISAF forces in Afghanistan. When I spoke with him, Gilbert cited a recent lost opportunity to turn things around in Palestine. He believed that when Obama was in Cairo he could have 'hopped aboard the Air Force One helicopter, flown to Gaza City and stepped out onto the balcony at Palestine Square and addressed the millions of Palestinians'. Then, in front of the massed millions, he could

[43]Harriet Sherwood, 'Doctor Mads Gilbert on working under siege in Gaza's Shifa hospital', *Guardian*, 23 June 2015.

have said, 'I am a Palestinian, like Kennedy did in Berlin when he said, *Ich bin ein Berliner*, I am a Berliner. *That could have changed history.*'

I'm personally not so sure. It would have been a poignant and emotional moment, but I suspect that nothing would have changed.

Israeli Foreign Ministry spokesman Yigal Palmor responded to the *Lancet* report by criticising Gilbert for 'spreading vicious lies'. In statements to the Associated Press, Palmor claimed, 'Dr Gilbert is notorious for his radical far left opinions and his systematic demonisation of Israel. He has already accused Israel of almost every nightmarish crime in the book only to ignore the refutation of every one of his allegations.' In a response to these statements Gilbert argued that he was the victim of a propaganda war.

Citing 'security reasons', Israel reportedly imposed a lifetime ban on Gilbert from entering Israel and entering the Gaza Strip from the Israeli border after the publication of the *Lancet* letter, which was undersigned by 24 doctors and scientists, in which it was argued that Israel was adopting the rhetoric of a national emergency to disguise the massacre of Palestinians, especially targeting women and children during the 2014 siege of Gaza.

This decision by the Israeli government sparked outrage in Norway and an official protest by the Norwegian government. On behalf of the government, Under-Secretary of State in the Foreign Ministry Bård Glad Pedersen said that 'Gilbert has for many years played an important role in assisting the Palestinian health care system, and his travels to Gaza are vital to continue this work.'

The Israeli government later explained that the ban imposed on Gilbert did not regard the Gaza Strip, but rather Israel, where his presence is regarded as constituting a security problem, and that the ban on entering Israel is not necessarily permanent. However, given the Egyptian closure of the Rafah passage, the only way to access the Gaza Strip is via an Israeli point of entry. Confusingly, Emmanuel Nachson, spokesperson for the Israeli Foreign Ministry, then claimed that Gilbert was 'welcome in Israel', contradicting other Israeli claims.

When I spoke with Gilbert he was determined, somehow or other, to find ways to continue his work in Gaza. It's worth recording, almost in full, an open letter he wrote on 22 July 2014, after witnessing the horror that he encountered:

Last night was extreme. The 'ground invasion' of Gaza resulted in scores and carloads with maimed, torn apart, bleeding, shivering, dying… All sorts of injured Palestinians, all ages, all civilians, all innocent. The heroes in the ambulances and in all of Gaza's hospitals are working 12 to 24-hour shifts, grey from fatigue and inhuman workloads (without payment in Shifa for the last four months). They care, triage, try to understand the incomprehensible chaos of bodies, sizes, limbs, walking, not walking, breathing, not breathing, bleeding, not bleeding humans… Now, once more treated like animals by 'the most moral army in the world' [sic!]. My closeness to the Palestinian 'sumud' [steadfastness] gives me strength, although in glimpses I just want to scream, hold someone tight, cry, smell the skin and hair of the warm child, covered in blood, protect ourselves in an endless embrace – but we cannot afford that, nor can they. We still have lakes of blood on the floor in the emergency room, piles of dripping, blood-soaked bandages to clear out…[and]…the cleaners are everywhere, swiftly shovelling the blood and discarded tissues, hair, clothes, cannulas – the leftovers from death – all taken away, to be prepared again, to be repeated all over. More than 100 cases came to Shifa in the last 24 hours. Enough for a large well-trained hospital with everything, but here, almost nothing: electricity, water, disposables, drugs, operating-room tables, instruments, monitors – all rusted and as if taken from museums of yesterday's hospitals. And as I write these words to you, alone, on a bed, my tears flow, the warm but useless tears of pain and grief, of anger and fear…[then]…the orchestra of the Israeli war-machine starts its gruesome symphony again. Just now: salvos of artillery from the navy boats down on the shores, the roaring F-16, the sickening drones and the Apaches. So much made by and paid for by the US. Mr Obama, do you have a heart? I invite you to spend one night, just one night, with us in Shifa. I am convinced, 100 per cent, it would change history. Nobody with a heart and power could ever walk away from a night in Shifa without being determined to end the slaughter of the Palestinian people.[44]

*

My heart is moved when listening to Gilbert. I contrast the bloody description of injury and death at the hands of the well-oiled and psychopathic Israeli war machine with the dignity of the Palestinians I know and about whom I learn. But, as I have repeatedly said, part of the cause is the way in which the Arab states refuse to aid the

---

[44]'Israel-Gaza conflict: Doctor Mads Gilbert evokes conditions in a Gaza hospital', *Independent*, 20 July 2014.

Palestinians and address their injustice. And what an injustice! Their homeland has been occupied!

Until Arabs stand firm and strong, Israel will continue to behave in any way it sees fit. An additional problem is that Palestinian leaders, like Abu Mazen (Mahmoud Abbas), the president of the State of Palestine, are weak and elicit suspicion. For example, many of these leaders possess substantial properties in countries like Scotland, send their children to prestigious Western schools and universities, such as St Andrews University, near Edinburgh, and the question may well be asked: where is the money coming from that funds these properties and expensive education? It is evident that many of these PLO and Fatah politicians and supporters possess extraordinary amounts of cash. Conversely, the politicians who represent Hamas appear closer to the Palestinian people and seem more transparent and honest.

And consider recent Egyptian politics: I remain shocked and saddened over the demise of the late president, Mohamed Morsi, who served as the fifth president of Egypt for just over a year, from 30 June 2012 to 3 July 2013, when he was then unceremoniously removed by army chief General Abdel Fattah el-Sisi after the June 2013 Egyptian protests and the 2013 Egyptian coup d'état. He had been the first democratically elected head of state in Egyptian history.

I ask the question: why didn't they give him a few more years? I know the answer: *this is the Arab way*. So we have to stop continuously blaming the West.

*

Let me return to Palestine. As I have repeatedly suggested, this injustice is at the core of the Middle Eastern psychosis. I am not alone in believing that there'll only be hope once the injustice is settled to the satisfaction of the Palestinians. Raja Shehadeh also believes there are grounds for hope, 'but only if the core problem, the Palestine problem, is resolved on grounds that allow equality between Israelis and Palestinians and for the Palestinians to enjoy their own state', because only then 'could the deadly fuse that was ignited more than a hundred years ago and which has been slowly burning further and further afield, setting off many bombs along its route over the large region of the Middle East, be extinguished.'[45]

Shehadeh argues that any satisfactory solution would then lead to the possibility for movement between, and cooperation among, the countries of the region. As he argues:

> The Middle East is not meant to be fragmented…[as]…the different parts of the region complement each other and would derive huge benefits in every sphere from the interaction between them. In some there is capital, in others labour. Here empty land, there congestion. Here an excess of educated people, there a need for teachers and professionals…[and]…from the interaction would arise many benefits from a rich cultural and religious mix, bringing a new cosmopolitanism rooted in our history. The region would go back to acting as the bridge between East and West as it has done for many centuries in the past.[46]

But none of this can happen as long as the borders remain closed, as long as the conflict is unresolved and the security of Israel is used as

[45]Raja Shehadeh, 'Palestine and Hope', in Raja Shehadeh and Penny Johnson, eds (2015), *Shifting Sands*, London: Profile Books, p. 245.
[46]*Ibid.*, p. 246.

an excuse to continue Western military interventions and restrictions on the Palestinian people.

In the conclusion to his magisterial history of the occupation, Ahron Bregman also believes there are grounds for hope, but sees it as more of something like a reluctant inevitability, and argues that he has 'little doubt that the occupation will come to an end at some point in the future, as all wars and conflicts do'.[47]

He reminds us that, in 1967, no one would have thought that Israel, Egypt and Jordan would have signed full peace treaties, and argues that it is reasonable to expect similar agreements to be signed, at some point, between Israel and the Palestinians and between Israel and Syria and Lebanon. But Bregman is realistic enough to add the rider that 'given the depth of the bad blood between the parties, particularly the Israelis and Palestinians, and the current revolutions in the Middle East, which distract from the conflict with Israel, it could take many generations before a true reconciliation takes hold'.[48]

It is perhaps worth allowing Bregman the last word in this summary of the Palestinian conflict, one that has shaped my parents' and, therefore, my life. He believes that the verdict of history will regard the four decades of Israeli occupation:

...as a black mark in Israeli and, indeed, Jewish history. This was a period in which Israel, helped by the Jewish diaspora, particularly in America, proved that even nations which have suffered

---

[47]Ahron Bregman (2014), *Cursed Victory: A History of Israel and the Occupied Territories*, London: Allen Lane, p. 306.
[48]*Ibid.*, p. 307.

unspeakable tragedies of their own can act in similarly cruel ways when in power themselves.[49]

Bregman somewhat poignantly observes that Israel never really thought it had any 'duty to help or protect the people under its control or to improve the quality of their lives', regarding them, at most, as a ready source of cheap labour. But of course this callous mistreatment of the Palestinians backfired and, as he concludes, by forcing them to live in squalor and without hope, 'Israel hardened those under its power, making them more determined to put an end to the occupation, by violent means if necessary, and live a life of dignity and freedom.'[50]

---

[49]*Ibid.*, p. 308.
[50]*Ibid.*

10

The South Pole & Onwards

Look not at my exterior form, but take what is in my hand.
JALĀL AD-DĪN MUHAMMAD RŪMĪ

A man who stands for nothing will fall for anything.
MALCOLM X

I mentioned making a film in 2015 with Robert Mullan. One of the obvious locations I suggested, to enhance the film's visual quality, was that of Wadi Rum, also known as the valley of the Moon, a landscape cut into the sandstone and granite rock of Southern Jordan. When I'm in Jordan I spend as much time there as I can, climbing, training for other kinds of expeditions, and just marvelling at its majesty and splendour.

In the West, Wadi Rum is probably best known for its connection with the British officer T. E. Lawrence, who passed through several times during the Arab revolt of 1917, and later it became a set for the film *Lawrence of Arabia*, based on his life. More recently, much of Ridley Scott's film *The Martian* was shot there. And indeed, there are times when it resembles something like a lunar landscape.

At night in Wadi Rum, sleeping in a Bedouin tent, avoiding the desert ants, I feel as if I am near to Allah. I am also in the place that,

at the time, radically altered the contours of the Middle East. I awake
in the middle of the night and look up and see the thousands of stars.
The Bedouin have climbed these mountains for many generations,
have lived here so long, yet they still haven't been properly provided
with schools for their children or adequate health support, especially
for their ageing population.

*

In 2015 I was participating in a Mosaic leadership conference in
Amman and took the opportunity to mention to another attendee,
the BBC's Head of Religious Programming, Aaqil Ahmed, that
I'd been involved in this documentary. I told him what had been
shot, who had been interviewed and the locations we'd travelled
to. For example, I mentioned that we'd covered the work of the
BDS movement, interviewed Mary Nazzal-Batayneh and Dr
Mads Gilbert, many refugees in Lebanon and Jordan, including
those Palestinians newly arrived from Syria, and so on, but by the
expression on his face I knew he was completely uninterested. I
must confess that I was not especially enthused by him: indeed, the
moment I first saw him I noted his facial features and demeanour,
and felt no love.

When I described the documentary he simply said, 'This isn't TV.'
Over a coffee later, he enthusiastically suggested an alternative which,
I surmised, he imagined I'd also enthusiastically embrace. His idea,
which he illustrated on a sheet of hotel notepaper, was that I take
two groups of young people – one Palestinian, the other Israeli – up
a mountain, 'any mountain', and encourage them, coax them, force
them to talk to each other. He thought such a 'show' would make

headlines and prove highly watchable. I immediately told him that I was a BDS supporter and that I boycotted all things Israeli, including young Israelis. I added that I had no interest in this. He argued that the 'show' would make a great contribution to the peace process between the two groups. I laughed and left the lobby of the hotel.

*

The film coincided with work I undertook for a charity, the Welfare Association (for Palestinian Refugees), and in particular for Salma elYassir, the Lebanese director of the organisation who had personally invited me. She strenuously works to try and alleviate the suffering of Palestinians in the various Lebanese refugee camps, and also to raise the visibility of their plight.

The Syrian conflict has sent over one million Syrian refugees, some of them Palestinian, across the border into Lebanon. They join half a million long-standing refugees who arrived in the 1940s from Palestine. No country has a higher proportion of refugees than Lebanon, with twelve Palestinian refugee camps, including three in Beirut. This small country of fewer than five million inhabitants has taken in over 1.5 million refugees and, as a result, has put the EU and others to shame. Jordan too has taken its fair share.

As I write, one of the greatest migrations ever seen is taking place throughout the Middle East and Europe. With very few legal and safe routes overland, many thousands of refugees are embarking on perilous sea journeys. Often making the trip towards Europe on flimsy and crowded dinghies, they are risking and sometimes losing their lives in the attempt. At least 2,600 people are thought to have died at sea in 2015 alone. Increasingly, women and children are among those endangered in what has become the worst refugee crisis since the Second World War.

In many places, local services are straining to meet the needs of the vulnerable people arriving. For example, on the Greek island of Lesbos, refugees are sheltered in hastily established transit camps run by local volunteers. Those that cannot be accommodated in the swelling camps sleep on the streets. All struggle to access basic services and lack even basic yet essential items such as blankets and soap. At the same time, NGOs like Islamic Relief continue to support refugees in countries such as Iraq, Jordan, Lebanon and Turkey.

Turkish authorities report that their coastguards rescued more than 42,000 people from the Aegean Sea in the first five months of 2015. Most of those trying to reach safety in Europe are fleeing the brutal conflict in Syria. Some 508,000 migrants made the perilous journey to reach Europe's shores in 2015 and over 300,000 in 2016, according to figures released by the International Organization for Migration (IOM).

Galip Kurdi, aged five, and his three-year-old brother Aylan died along with their mother, Rehan, and 10 other refugees when their boat capsized as they were trying to reach the Greek island of Kos. The family was fleeing Kobane in Syria, which so-called Islamic State (Isis) has recently attacked. The children's father, Abdullah, survived. His sister, Teema Kurdi, told the *Ottawa Citizen* that the family had a G5 privately sponsored application for asylum in Canada rejected by Citizenship and Immigration in June of this year. Teema, who emigrated to Canada 20 years ago, was trying to sponsor them, and with friends and neighbours paid the bank deposits but couldn't get them out, which is why they went in the boat. The Canadian

Citizenship and Immigration Department said that the family couldn't be granted asylum because the UN wouldn't register them as refugees, and the Turkish government wouldn't grant them exit visas because they didn't have passports.

I despair, and in the absence of a global decision to abandon all borders and issue international passports, I have no idea how this crisis can be solved. In the meantime, countries such as Lebanon and Jordan will take the pressure while the UK, various Eastern European countries and, of course, the USA, will abdicate responsibility.

In addition to this, I feel that if refugees were able to find a safe haven in Saudi Arabia, the UAE or Qatar, helped by their fellow Muslims, they would not be forced to make the suicidal journey to Europe.

*

The Shatila (also known as Chatila) camp in southern Beirut has been home to refugees since 1949. Its population has swelled from 9,000 to almost 20,000, due in part to Palestinians recently fleeing Syria. Over half of the refugees are jobless and others have work that is difficult to secure, precarious and always low paid. In Shatila, children walk to school through dark alleyways, where sewage flows in open drains under their feet, and where thousands of broken electrical cables hang down and occasionally cause death by electrocution. Some of these alleyways resemble a medieval ghetto, a backwards glance at history. There are no gardens to be seen, no flowers to be cultivated and no trees to climb, shade under or simply enjoy.

Schools, catering for all age groups, and other educational resources are rare in the camps, although each camp varies in its level of provision. In Lebanon, overall school dropout rates for Palestinian children over 10 years of age are well over 40 per cent. Nonetheless, among Palestinians, belief in education remains strong. It's seen by many, if not all, as one of the major routes out of their situation.

Walking around Shatila I was amazed and saddened at the degree of damp and poor hygiene that plagues most homes. Half of all households have water leaking through ceilings or walls, and severe overcrowding appears common. One area I walked through was originally designed as a playground for children of all ages to play in, but has now degenerated into a rubbish dump, dangerous and highly toxic.

Almost three-quarters of all Palestinian refugees living in Lebanon cannot afford to meet their minimal food and nutritional requirements, and are categorised by various health authorities as 'poor or very poor'. Poverty, substandard housing and unhealthy environments are directly related to the prevalence of disease among Palestinian children, and I was told that over one-third of Palestinian refugees suffer from chronic illnesses. I certainly met and spoke with many unwell children.

Rising rents, increased competition for scarce jobs, and lower daily wages for those fortunate enough to get any kind of work, however precarious, are some of the consequences of the recent massive influx of Palestinian refugees from Syria.

As a Palestinian, accompanied by Salma elYassir, it was easy and enjoyable walking around the Shatila camp. I passed the time of day with old men, played football with children in the narrow alleyways, and tasted food from one of the many refugee-owned small businesses. Nonetheless, political posters and slogans abound, and on the streets there's endless political talk.

In fact, the somewhat calm outward appearance of the camp masks its tragic history as, in 1982, these very same streets were covered in blood and corpses after a two-day massacre. After Israeli armed forces closed the exits to the camp, Christian Phalangist militias killed approximately three thousand civilians. Illuminating flares fired into the air by the Israeli army allowed the Phalangists to hunt their victims far into the night. Following a special Israeli investigation, personal responsibility for the massacre was attributed to Ariel Sharon, which subsequently forced him to resign as Defence Minister.

I talked with a 91-year-old survivor, Abdulallah Taleb Salhani, who still lives in Shatila and who still remembers the killings, including the night his only son was murdered. The only thing he has left of his son is the dried blood on the knife that mercilessly killed him. Unlike the people I was with in the camp, who believed totally in the role of education in changing the future, this man saw things completely differently: 'What's been taken by force can only be taken back by force.'

*

Working in Lebanon was fulfilling. I'd previously been to Beirut, when it was the clubbing capital of the world, but had never been to any of the camps.

Beirut was torn apart in the vicious civil war that finally ended in 1990 and which claimed over 150,000 lives. Even today, in 2015, bullet and shrapnel holes mark the majority of the older buildings, but the city has 'moved on', and feels more relaxed and unashamedly wealthy. Indeed, million-dollar apartments populate the downtown area and the distinctive art-deco clock tower has Rolex written on its face. After a multi-billion-dollar reconstruction project, the city centre boasts upmarket cafés, refurbished Ottoman-era buildings and boutiques, favouring Hermès, Burberry and Versace.

I really loved working with young Palestinian refugees in Lebanon. My task was to try and engage with and inspire these youthful refugees, in the hope that they might engage more with education and resist any temptation to join the extremist groups that recruit. The temptation is always present: it's difficult to drive anywhere in the country without encountering checkpoints, militia, posters and propaganda from Hezbollah, and other groups, and in the camps themselves there are constant attempts at recruitment by the various factions of Fatah, Hamas and the PLO.

I related to the teenagers I worked with. I knew how they felt, because once I also felt stateless, vulnerable and unwanted. In Jordan, Palestinians are given passports, unlike in Lebanon. In Jordan there was the available spare land, and the Palestinians brought to the country a desired entrepreneurial mentality and numerous small businesses. But in Lebanon these young Palestinians have nothing, no education, no study, no employment or work, no passport, *no hope*.

So one narrative is that some of these young people leave school, or some kind of further or higher education, then immediately become unemployed, and then pick up a gun. Of the kids that I worked with in Lebanon, 50 per cent didn't care at all about what I said to them. I think I positively affected 10 – about half, or a little less – of those I worked with. Despite returning home and leaving them in their camps, I still receive numerous messages on Facebook and WhatsApp. The messages they send me say things like, 'I found my own Everest after I met you.' One guy said, 'I'll follow my own Everest, and try and become a maths teacher.' Others told me that they'd studied harder after I spoke with them and had received over 70 per cent in their exams, which meant the UN would pay for their higher education.

Some of them now think they have a different and possibly better future. These young people want to believe. What they see in me is someone like them, who also came from a camp, yet didn't give up or turn to violence or despair but, instead, did something with his life.

Talking to some of these young people – the less engaged among them – reminded me that the real danger is when young Muslims travel to Syria and other combat zones, then return home to the UK, Belgium, France or elsewhere. They're often not Arabs but, for example, homegrown British or Belgian mercenaries. When I encounter disillusioned young Muslims in Europe, especially Britain, I say to them, 'If you want to live a life in a truly Muslim nation, leave, go there, go to Malaysia or somewhere.' Or, 'You can stay in the UK where you're free to practise your religion, and say almost anything you want to.' But I also say to such disaffected youth, 'If you want to be a good Muslim, don't fight unless you are attacked or you have to save your family or country. Be kind and be honest. Respect other religions. We all worship the same God. There's no need to convert or change anyone. Just accept everyone.'

With the Palestinian kids in Lebanon I simply tell them my story. They usually have little hope for their future. Of course, their lives are very different to the nightmare of their parents' past, but they still know that the odds remain stacked against them. For example, Palestinians who want to go to university face many obstacles, and even if they pass exams and graduate, they will invariably have to somehow leave Lebanon to find any kind of work. This absence of opportunity leads many to drop out of school.

My work entails leading hiking expeditions with those kids who are reluctant or refusing to attend school. I take them to beautiful places, like Jezzine, one of Lebanon's most well-known districts. All around are mountain peaks and pine forests. We walk and then, as casually as possible, I find a way of speaking with each of them on a one-to-one basis, and offer understanding and advice. They tell me their life stories, of the misfortune that has befallen their families, of the appalling conditions they live in.

I try and motivate them by being realistic. I don't simply show them videos of me at the North Pole or on Everest or Kilimanjaro and say, 'I did it, so can you.' No, I get a sense of what they are interested in – and many aren't interested in anything – then set them short-, medium- and long-term goals. I tell them that is what I did for my Everest climbs: begin with a 5,000-metre climb, then 6,000, and then 7,000. And, I say, if you want to be an astronaut and fly to the moon, your short-term goal would be to learn physics.

Risks should be calculated. To take the example of my 2015–2016 expedition to the South Pole: I trained and also secured my family's future. I take full responsibility, and find the required finance and train. So if I die on the expedition at least I know I have tried my best and reduced the risk.

With these kids I show them how hard it was to prepare for and to climb Everest. I describe the necessary qualities of patience, stamina, mental fortitude and willpower. It's also good to be able to tell them that twice I failed to summit Everest *but didn't give up*. Perhaps that's the best lesson of all.

I inject humour into this educational process when I allow someone to experience the cumbersome, but essential, clothing I wore to reach the summit, and this seems to break the ice and engage them further.

*

Outside the refugee camps, some groups of Palestinians live in ramshackle buildings built without official permission. These are known as 'gatherings'. Jal El Baher is one such community, south of Beirut, by the sea and home to a group of fishermen. It was established in 1948 and suffered bombings in both 1982 and 2006, but somehow it remains. I played football with the children who have to play along the shoreline, amid a mass of refuse and rubbish. The local authority provides few or no services to these ramshackle shelters, which barely offer their inhabitants protection from the elements. When the weather deteriorates, so do their lives, as water enters their shelters and contributes to their ill health.

Indeed, vulnerability to a variety of health problems is evident in both mothers and children living in these exceptionally difficult circumstances. Nonetheless, many of these young children appear resilient in the face of these extremely stressful living conditions.

When I was in the camp, I was told an absolutely heartbreaking story. A seven-year-old boy, who lived in appalling conditions, was desperate to attend a school, to learn to read and write, and so he decided to cross a busy road each day to reach a small but amenable public school. After four happy days, this small boy returned home, started to cross the road, was hit by a lorry and died.

*

On my southern journey I also travelled 3 km east of the historic city of Tyre, to the Burj el-Shemali camp. This camp was also established in 1948, after the first Arab-Israeli War, and it was only ever intended to be a temporary home. However, it now holds almost twenty thousand registered refugees and like all the other Lebanese camps it has experienced a recent influx of Palestinian refugees from Syria. Kasem Aina administers the Beit Atfal Assumoud, a centre designed to assist young Palestinians. He told me a brief version of his life story, which starts in 1948, when he and his family of eight had to flee their home in Alma. He remembers that he was asleep in bed when a 'warplane flew overhead'. The villagers, unused to the sound of such a plane, fled their homes. Kasem – now an enthusiastic and healthy 70-year-old – says that his mother, in a panic, picked up a pillow instead of him! She took refuge in a vineyard outside of the village, and was startled when one of her daughters asked, 'Where's Kasem?' Luckily, Kasem's mother defied the bombs and returned to collect him.

As I walked around the Burj el-Shemali camp with Kasem I was struck by how Palestinian identity is a source of pride and passion, among both the young and old. Palestinians I met at Burj el-Shemali, like everywhere else, still believe in the right of return. No one throws away the keys to their old houses or the fading title deeds to their old lands. Palestinian refugees have been dispersed to 22 host countries, in which they are often told to 'go back from where they came'. They respond, 'We too have a homeland and none of us will renounce the right of return whatever it costs.' The sentiment appears to be that, 'even though I am a Palestinian refugee and my children were born outside their own country, I still raised them to love Palestine and to draw Palestine's map in their hearts so they'll never forget'.

*

When I'm in Amman I often recall the late King Hussein. He was intelligent and kindly, which could be seen in his face. He had the ability to talk to emperors, chefs or peasants. King Hussein also knew what was going on throughout all parts of his country.

Whenever I return to Jordan, I also visit the grave of my late Sufi teacher, Shaykh Mamdouh abu Shamat. As well as learning the Qur'an, I learned much from his teaching about Sufism's mystical and peaceful path, and about building bridges between different beliefs and people. As far as I'm concerned, Sufism's concentration on awareness and psychological balance, or mindfulness, makes it a natural antidote to religious fanaticism.

Sufism totally and completely affects the way I live my life. I live the best I can like a Sufi, which means that I concentrate and focus. I have passion and always fall in love with my projects. I try and take opportunities to take myself away from the material world. I practise my religion and pray and meditate. Praying five times a day *is* a meditation and is not so different from Buddhist practice. It makes me feel exhilarated, and when I join a Sufi circle I feel absolute joy.

Shaykh Ali, from Kashmir, completely changed my life. He gave me my first taste of Sufism. People used to kiss his hand and I continued that tradition by kissing my Jordanian shaykh's hand, out of respect. Whenever I have sought advice from a shaykh, I listen, respectfully, but make up my own mind. I don't simply follow. I live my own life. I design my own life. There's only one judge, Allah.

I live with one foot in the Arab world, and one in the West. What I admire and enjoy in the Arab world centres around the strong emphasis placed on family and tradition. For instance, if anything happened to me and I was incapacitated or indeed dead, I know that my children would be taken care of and would be secure, because all my brothers would ensure it. What I don't admire about the Arab world is the existence of the numerous glass ceilings. The UK has given me opportunities the Arab world would never have done. In the Arab world even a genius would be 'taken down', and shown 'his place'. Conversely, in the Arab world if my father had been a minister I would have been rewarded far more than I have been. This isn't to suggest that I have an ego that requires massaging; rather, it would have been easier for me to work even more effectively for the benefit of various charities.

*

My latest challenge would rank among my final ones, and a huge one: an expedition to the South Pole. This would require being away from home for about two and a half months, skiing every day with a heavy sledge and limitless ice and snow as far as the eye can see. I hadn't trained or gained as much weight as I had hoped in preparation for the expedition, but nevertheless I was ultimately successful.

In the New Year of 2016, after 56 days in Antarctica and 40 days skiing, I made it to the South Pole and became the first ever Muslim and Arab to reach it through the Messner route (named after the explorer Reinhold Messner). The Jordanian and Palestinian flags flew at the southernmost point of the earth as they had done in 2008 on top of the world. In reaching the South Pole, I completed the 'Grand Slam' of mountaineering and polar adventure, becoming one of only thirteen people in the world to do so.

This was the culmination of an enormous amount of hard work. Fund-raising is one of the aspects of my work in which I excel but which is, nonetheless, tiring and stressful. Raising money is time-consuming and ultimately serendipitous. Targeted financiers or sponsors change their minds or prove to be unhelpful, whereas 'long shots' often deliver finance speedily and without question. Perseverance and tenacity are important qualities for anyone involved in fund-raising.

For the South Pole expedition I spent many stressful months in the search for money and sponsorship. Just recently a very good friend of mine, who is a spiritual teacher in Jordan, Eman Suhiemat, put me in touch with his brother Mohammed's best friend, who in turn is the brother of a man named Ziad Al Manaseer. I told Al Manaseer what I needed and it took five minutes; he said he would be honoured to sponsor me to take the Jordanian flag to the South Pole and spread the message of good Islam. I found this deeply touching. Al Manaseer, Chairman of the Manaseer Group, one of Jordan's largest companies, with interests in many sectors including energy and chemicals, agreed to be one of my main sponsors, and Umniah again agreed to participate, as did the Landmark Hotel Amman, Palma Holding, Dubai and Toyota, Jordan. The expedition costs include equipment purchase, travel, the cost of upkeep of my Dublin home while I'm away, and so on. I was greatly helped in preparing for the expedition by Helen Turton, one of the world's best polar guides, who trained me for the South Pole and helped me to secure the best equipment available.

Having completed the South Pole, I hope I am able to inspire Muslims all over the world to follow my example, my *jihad*.

Aspley Cherry-Garrard's memoir of the 1910–13 British Antarctic Expedition, led by Robert Falcon Scott, was titled *The Worst Journey in the World*.[1] It's a frank account of Scott's expedition, which unfortunately overshadowed the first successful one by Roald Engelbregt Gravning Amundsen, the Norwegian explorer who led the Antarctic expedition of 1910–12 which reached the South Pole on 14 December 1911. The author, who was a member of Scott's team, writes of the great sacrifices involved in polar exploration, particularly to the South Pole, where team members must be able to contemplate 'loss with equanimity (even to the point of suicide, if one suffers a serious, disabling accident)', where they must 'accept starvation as part of the price of admission to an exclusive club, not only with regard to food, but also sexual and social starvation', and where they 'must determine what they can physically withstand'.[2]

Kari Herbert and Huw Lewis-Jones, in a preface to their 'visual essay' on the South Pole, describe the place in startling terms:

This is a world that offers no welcome. There are places on this frozen continent where your footprints will outlive you…[and]… it is a landscape of the imagination, a region of the heart's desire. It is a place where ambitions can run riot; where energy, and vanity, can freeze in an instant; and where the best-laid plans surrender to a turn in the weather. It is a place from which some never return…[and]…it is a dull, empty and featureless place where dismay seeps into your skin…[and]…humans go there at their peril.[3]

[1]Aspley Cherry-Garrard (1922), *The Worst Journey in the World*, London: Constable & Co.
[2]Ross D. E. MacPhee (2010), *Race to the End: Scott, Amundsen and the South Pole*, London: The Natural History Museum, p. 214.
[3]Kari Herbert and Huw Lewis-Jones (2011), *In Search of the South Pole*, London: Conway, pp. 9–10.

My journey entailed the hauling of considerable supplies, facing constant winds, encountering fields of *sastrugi* (sharp, irregular grooves or ridges formed on a snow surface by wind erosion, saltation of snow particles, and sediment – *eroded snow*) and also 'whiteout' conditions, where the horizon disappears completely.

From Punta Arenas, Chile, accompanied by a guide Devon McDiarmid and two fantastic team-mates Stewart Edge and Shahrom Abdullah, we flew for something like five hours to Antarctica. There are two possible routes to the South Pole: the Hercules route, at 1,170 kilometres (730 miles), which is slightly longer, and the Messner option, a little shorter at 934 kilometres (580 miles). There is a gradual climb to more than 2,800 metres (9,300 feet) as the team moved south over the ice cap's mountain passes and windblown snow ridges. My days were filled with 24-hour daylight and an intense solitude and tranquillity. No plant or animal life is seen that far south, just snow, ice, rock and sky.

The favoured route was inspired by Reinhold Messner's 1989 crossing. He, of course, is the legendary mountaineer, explorer and one-time MEP for the Italian Green Party. We skiied through remote, unexplored terrain, from the Ronne Ice Shelf on the edge of the frozen Antarctic continent to the geographic South Pole. The physiological altitude exceeds 3,350 metres (11,000 feet) for many days in a row, and temperatures may drop below –40°F / –40°C, with severe wind chill and storms. As I said, the trip takes around two and a half months, or some 50 days on the ice, depending on the snow conditions and the team dynamic. The team skiied for about 8–12 hours a day in all types of weather and in challenging terrain, all the time hauling sleds weighing 80–90 kg (175–200 lbs).

I completed the South Pole for numerous reasons and causes: for His Majesty King Abdullah and for Jordan, for Al Rayeh Al Hashmieh (the Hashemite flag), Islam, the King Hussein Cancer Center and Osama Yaseen, and for all my sponsors and my family. I did it too for the little boy who sent me a toy helicopter, gifts such as these spur me on. Blustered, frostbitten, broken, tired, exhausted but never bowed, I made it.

While training for the expedition I realised that I actually wanted to create a new route to the South Pole, a route that I can put my name to, again for the benefit of the Muslim world. Not just to create a route that's never before been walked and have my name attached, but to raise awareness of peaceful Islam. So, along with three other explorers from Ireland and the USA, we've come up with a new route which, although still an 'idea', I hope will come to fruition in the near future.

This new route would take about 60 days and involves travel over crevasses, so any participants would require solid mountaineering experience. No one has ever walked the route we're proposing. We'll be approaching from the north. In my more philosophical moments, I realise that no one has ever prayed on the snow that we'll encounter. We will be helped in our planning by NASA, and their satellite data.

The proposed new route will take years to train for and plan. Equipment will have to be sourced, flights from Chile to Antarctica negotiated, and two training sessions in Norway organised. The costs include a contingency for emergencies, and, of course, the company that provides the major elements of the expedition takes almost 50 per cent of the costs. But it's a team idea and I am merely the producer.

Any of the South Pole routes – Hercules, Messner or the new planned route – are potentially hazardous, as Scott and others discovered. I've read a lot about earlier explorers and mountaineers, and compared with the technology I possess they had nothing. But as much as this new technology helps, any explorer or climber still has to possess mental strength. To keep up my mental strength and positivity on the 2016 journey I took two books to the Pole with me: Oprah Winfrey's *What I Know For Sure* and Paulo Coelho's *The Alchemist*. As I've mentioned before, Coelho's book has a special importance for me in particular.

Another item in my diary is a climb in Russia, as part of my 'From the Lowest Point to the Highest Point' brand of charitable climbs. It will be a climb for Circassian children and also child victims of war. The team, who I'll select, will travel from Jordan's Dead Sea to Mount Elbrus, the highest mountain in Russia and the Caucasus Range, near the Georgian border. Elbrus, which peaks at 5,642 metres (18,510 feet), is the tenth-highest mountain in the world. The planned climb has already proven popular and over twenty people from the Jordanian Caucasus have shown a desire to participate.

Interestingly, Mount Elbrus and the Caucasus Range also divide Russia from the Middle East. Its name is believed to derive from *Alborz*, which in turn comes from *Harā Bərəzaitī*, a mountain in Persian mythology, translated as 'High Sentinel'. Elbrus also has other names in other languages, including *Mingi Tau*, which translates to 'Eternal Mountain', or *Oshkhamakhua*, 'Mountain of Happiness' in Circassian. Elbrus is perpetually snow-covered with an icecap and 22 glaciers, and is geologically considered an inactive volcano. Lava flows cover the mountain as well as 100 square miles of volcanic ash and debris. It last erupted around 50 AD.

Even with the new South Pole expedition and Elbrus to plan I will also be organising a trip taking a team of the first Jordanian women to climb Everest. They will come from all walks of life: from well-known Jordanian families, Christian communities, Palestinians and Muslims. We will train in the Himalayas, Tibet and South America before climbing Everest in 2018.

*

In addition to these trips, I also intend to perform *hajj*. This is very important for me, as it is for nearly all Muslims. Perhaps the most important journey any Muslim can undertake, its significance cannot be underestimated. Interestingly, I recently discovered that in the 1960s, the American Black Rights leader Malcolm X left the Nation of Islam movement after going on *hajj* and realising that white people could be fellow believers and brothers![4]

One of my favourite stories about *hajj* concerns Ibn Battuta, the fourteenth-century Moroccan traveller who spent 29 years on *hajj*. He began his travels in 1325, at the age of 20. His main reason to travel was to go on pilgrimage to Makkah, as all good Muslims should. However, and inadvertently, his travelling went on for 29 years and he covered about 75,000 miles, visiting the equivalent of 44 modern countries, which were then mostly under the governments of Muslim leaders (the region, 'Dar al-Islam'). On his travels he was allegedly attacked by bandits, almost drowned in a sinking ship, was almost beheaded by a tyrant ruler, and enjoyed a few marriages and lovers, fathering several children! Near the end of Ibn Battuta's life, the Sultan

---

[4]Kevin O'Donnell (2006), *Inside World Religions*, Banbury: Lion Books, p. 163.

of Morocco insisted that he dictate the story of his travels to a scholar so the world could learn of his remarkable life.[5]

A brief history of the *hajj* would perhaps start with the time when pagan Arabs came to Makkah (Mecca) each year on pilgrimage. They circled the *Ka'aba* (also *Ka'bah*) and offered sacrifices on the black stone (it has been speculated that this may have been a fertility ritual). Muhammad subsequently cleansed the *hajj* of pagan customs.

Hajj takes place during the twelfth Islamic month, and each year over two million Muslims make this pilgrimage to Makkah. Male pilgrims wear a white robe made of two sheets of unsewn cloth, and women pilgrims must be completely covered. The *hajj* lasts for five days, beginning with circling the *Ka'aba* ('first place of worship'/'the house of God') seven times, then the pilgrims go to two small hills nearby, and then time is spent in the valley of Arafat among special tents, meditating, and thereafter part of the evening is spent collecting 49 small stones.

After Mecca and Arafat the pilgrims gather in Mina, where it is believed Ishmael drove the devil away by throwing stones and, accordingly, the pilgrims throw stones as a symbol of turning away from evil.

Making *hajj* is very important for me. I'm not perfect and I'm not a saint, so this pilgrimage is necessary. It's a pillar of Islam, and I'm certain it will be another turning point. Yes, I'll finish both expeditions to the South Pole and then I'll make *hajj*. As I have a UK passport I can make *hajj* while I'm still relatively young. I make the point about

---

[5]See Ibn Battuta and Samuel Lee (transl.) (2004), *The Travels of Ibn Battuta: in the Near East, Asia and Africa, 1325–1354*, London: Dover Publications.

my British passport because if I used my Jordanian passport, and because of the quota system employed there, I would have to wait until I was about 65.

Mount Arafat (also Mount Arafah) is a granite hill on the plain of Arafat, about 20 km southeast of Makkah. It reaches about 70 metres (230 feet) in height and is also known as the Mount of Mercy (*Jabal ar-Rahmah*). It is believed to be the place where Prophet Muhammad Peace Be Upon Him stood and delivered the Farewell Sermon to the Muslims who accompanied him for the *hajj* towards the end of his life.

On *hajj* I want to help old and less-abled people. I want to give them money that I have and they don't. I want to help them up Mount Arafat, maybe carry someone to the top, bring them down and then take someone else to the top. I could even throw the stones for them.

I don't want to make *hajj* simply to 'wash my sins away'. I want to help other people who have saved for years for the journey to accomplish something they've spent all their lives trying to achieve.

*

Despite the love I hold for my faith, for the Prophet and for Allah, I remain profoundly open-minded towards all other religions and philosophies, and believe that an individual is entitled to take what they want from anywhere and construct their own belief system. For example, I greatly respect the central Buddhist notion of taking responsibility for one's own life. For a Buddhist there is no one to 'save us' and no one to take the blame for our poor decisions.

I want to be able to go into temples, churches, anywhere I want, where I can think, meditate, pray. There have always been interrelationships between all the major faiths: simply consider the case of Andalusian Sufism, in medieval Spain, which greatly influenced numerous Jews as well as Christians.

We cannot afford to be dogmatic about our religion. I shared a tent and an enjoyable journey to the North Pole with Fey, from China. He was enthusiastic about Islam, so I gave him a little taste of my religion, I didn't put any obstacles in his way.

Although India opened my heart to Islam, especially Sufism, previously I had loved Ramadan, this time of renewal and cleansing and the reduction and cessation of excess. And when in India, Hinduism also positively affected me. I would learn all about the beautiful songs which were unashamed and heartfelt pleas to God: 'I am a cleaner in a bank, and in the next life I want to be a bank manager', and a bank manager singing, 'I am a bank manager and in the next life I want to be a government official'. This really struck me. The mythology behind Hinduism was sweet.

I would sit on a houseboat in Kashmir and reflect that Judaism, Christianity and Islam have created chaos around the world, but, conversely, Buddhism, Hinduism and Sikhism, less so. So I decided to pray in a Sikh temple and loved it – loved the sense of mystery and community.

My life has been shaped by a number of people and books, and I always take the opportunity to pass anything I consider to be of value on to others. This is why I enjoy working with Palestinian youth, who I can try and inspire just by telling them the truth of my life. In 1997, I was given a copy of *The Alchemist* and it simply stated that 'you have to believe in yourself'. You have to create your own destiny. You must follow your dream. It is also about contentment. It is not about money, but respect. It changed my life.

I base my ideas and my teaching on what I've achieved. I'll also read Rumi, some speeches I've found in Shakespeare, Socrates, the lives of Einstein and Da Vinci, as well as other people who inspire me.

I was recently waiting for a train near Paddington Station, London, to take me to Heathrow and onwards to Amman. I drank some nice sweet Turkish coffee then spent an hour browsing in a second-hand bookshop. I picked up an old and musty paperback by Norman Vincent Peale, solely because of its title: *The Power of Positive Thinking*. I thought, 'This describes what I believe in!'

I later discovered that this was a bestseller way back in 1952, and on the back of this sun-faded paperback were some of the author's phrases and pieces of advice, including his assertion that the way to 'happiness' was to 'keep your heart free from hate, your mind from worry. Live simply, expect little, and give much. Scatter sunshine, forget self, and think of others.' And also, 'formulate and stamp indelibly on your mind a mental picture of yourself as succeeding. Hold this picture tenaciously. Never permit it to fade. Your mind will seek to develop the picture... Do not build up obstacles in your imagination.' Wow, I thought, 'this is what I believe, this is what I say to those kids I teach, this is what I do when I challenge myself.'

On the Heathrow Express I googled his name and discovered that Norman Vincent Peale was born in Ohio in 1898, and died in New York in 1993, at the age of 95. He was ordained a Methodist minister in 1922, but then changed his religious affiliation to the Reformed Church of America and began a 52-year tenure as pastor of Marble Collegiate Church in Manhattan. During his tenure the church's membership grew from 600 to over 5,000, and he became one of the city's most famous preachers. Then I read that, on hearing of Peale's death, former US President Bill Clinton remarked that:

> The name of Dr. Norman Vincent Peale will forever be associated with the wondrously American values of optimism and service. Dr. Peale was an optimist who believed that, whatever the antagonisms and complexities of modern life brought us, anyone could prevail by approaching life with a simple sense of faith. In a productive and giving life that spanned the twentieth century, Dr. Peale lifted the spirits of millions and millions of people who were nourished and sustained by his example, his teaching, and his giving. He will be missed.[6]

There is nothing in what Peale writes that I would disagree with – live simply, serve others, expect little, formulate plans and hold on to them. This short little book confirmed much of what I believe, about responsibility, about positivity, about human kindness. And, like me, Peale held a strong faith and believed in God's will.

*

Will my marriage survive a second South Pole? All this is difficult for my children and my wife in Dublin. I work hard in my relationships, whether it be with my sponsors, my team members on expeditions, the people I work with, my family both extended and nuclear, my children and Krissy, my wife. It is difficult for Krissy to construct a family life with an absent husband and father. My restlessness ensures that there is one challenge after another, and they all take me away

---

[6]Weekly Compilation of Presidential Documents, 1 March 1994.

from Dublin. And fund-raising also tends to take me away from Ireland.

In the past I did have lots of girlfriends, and indeed many good male friends too, and some of my friends would say that it was almost impossible for a woman to have a 'relationship' with me. I would have women friends both in the UK and abroad and was regularly accused of presenting a different version of myself to each of them. But I was also capable of regularly spoiling the women I was with: unlike some of my friends who would consider 'a date' a pint of lager after a trip to the cinema, I would prepare a picnic and take my companion up to Calton Hill in Edinburgh. I would often shower them with flowers.

I've tried hard to compromise because I love my family and want my marriage to prosper.

I've often been accused of being a romantic, especially with my idea of no longer climbing and, instead, opening a café in Edinburgh where I can make exotic sandwiches. Some people believe that maybe I will open such a place, but won't actually ever be there myself.

*

The human brain is made up of so many cells and if I keep telling myself that I cannot do this or that, then of course I won't, because I'm programming myself not to do so. But, if I say to myself, 'I *will* do this', if I look in the mirror in the morning and say 'I will do this' then I will.

If I did it, you can.

Being positive is what I teach. If I fail after being positive, so be it. What have I lost? Nothing. I just have to find a different way. But if I think negatively I would simply give up or not even start.

People often ask why I was the only person in my family to achieve in the way that I have. It's simply that I wanted the change. However, it also came to me. My intentions were good. I learned English. I developed my own courage.

When I develop an idea or a project, I visualise. I use that side of my brain. I also have to stand by my principles. This is why I'm always careful who I take money from to fund my trips.

*

The only thing that is written for me, by Allah, and about which I can do nothing to alter, is the timing of my death – the day, the minute, the second I die. I believe that because of my faith, which has allowed me to live freely and have peace of mind. When on the mountain, I never fear death, because it is already written for me – besides, far more people die on the roads daily than ever do on the mountain.

Allah knows all about my destiny, knows what is going to happen in the life I have created and continue to create.

I am proud to be a Muslim, and sometimes proud to be an Arab, especially for what they did in the twelfth and fourteenth centuries. Faith in Allah gives me peace. Allah is always with me on the mountain. And when I'm in any kind of trouble, I go back to Allah.

*

Perhaps it's a paradox, but when I'm alone on the mountain it is blissful, yet when I'm back on terra firma I don't enjoy being alone. I am a people person.

When I climb I get away from the repetitive and mundane domesticity of everyday life. I like being on my own. But climbing is not the passion of my life. The passion of my life is changing other people's lives, by teaching, mentoring, telling people my story in order to try and inspire them, raising money for charities, taking people up mountains they'd never dreamed of climbing, in fact helping people climb for the very first time in their lives.

*

For legendary Sherpa Tenzing Norgay, 'the pull of Everest was stronger for me than any force on earth', so much so that in 1947 he even participated in a clandestine trip to the mountain through Tibet with solitary Anglo-Canadian climber Earl Denman.[7] By 1953, Tenzing had spent more time on Everest than any other human being, a fact which the British were well aware of, which is why he was one of the mainstays of their attempt on the mountain and crucial to the expedition's success. In 2011 his son, Jamling, offered the following observation:

> In the mountains, worldly attachments are left behind, and in the absence of material distractions, we are opened up to spiritual thought ...[and]...we should be attempting to carry the spiritual experience of the mountains with us everywhere.[8]

[7]Huw Lewis-Jones (2011), *Mountain Heroes*, London: Conway, p. 184.
[8]*Ibid.*, p. 275.